What Brings You to Life?

What Brings You to Life?

Awakening Woman's Spiritual Essence

Beverly E. Eanes

Lee J. Richmond

and

Jean W. Link

Paulist Press
New York/Mahwah, New Jersey

The Publisher gratefully acknowledges use of the following: Excerpt from *Guide My Feet* by Marian Wright Edelman, © 1995 by Marian Wright Edelman. Reprinted by permission of Beacon Press, Boston. Unless otherwise noted, the Scripture quotations contained herein are from the New Revised Standard Version Bible, copyright © 1989 by the Division of Christian Education of the National Council of the Churches in the U.S.A., and are used by permission. All rights reserved.

Cover design by Cynthia Dunne
Interior design by Lynn Else

Library of Congress Cataloging-in-Publication Data

Eanes, Beverly Elaine.
     What brings you to life : awakening woman's spiritual essence / Beverly E. Eanes, Lee J. Richmond, and Jean W. Link.
        p. cm.
     Includes bibliographical references.
     ISBN 0-8091-4045-4 (alk. paper)
     1. Woman—Religious life. 2. Self-esteem in women—Religious aspects.
     I. Richmond, Lee Joyce, 1934- II. Link, Jean W. III. title.

     BL625.7.E355 2001
     291.4'4'082—dc21

                                                             2001045804

Published by
PAULIST PRESS
997 Macarthur Boulevard
Mahwah, New Jersey 07430

www.paulistpress.com

Printed and bound in the United States of America

Contents

Dedication

To all the wise and caring women who have gone before us,

Illuminating our pathways...

And, to those women coming after us who see the reflections,

That highlight their own essence...

Of WomanSoul

Acknowledgments

Each of the authors has been through difficult circumstances while writing *What Brings You to Life?* These struggles slowed us down but did not count us out. Irregardless of our own determination, we also received much support from family, friends, students and coworkers who believed in awakening women's spiritual essence.

We are grateful to Maria Maggi, managing editor of Paulist Press, who, even through her own difficult circumstances, continued to encourage us during this long gestational process.

We are indebted to many staff members of Loyola College in Maryland for their support, especially June August and A. J. Tepe, for their interest and attention to detail.

Lee gives thanks to the creative and determined people in her stories and to the women who helped her with her research studies for this book.

Jean would like to thank her husband, Don, for his incredible support as well as "confidence in my writing that helped me believe in myself, especially as an author."

Bev is very grateful to her husband, Dave, for his stalwart support, accepting spirit, caring critique and, above all, his loving presence.

Our special thanks goes to the many women of all ages, near and far, who spoke to us candidly and with much enthusiasm, and sometimes with pleasant surprises about what brings them to life!

Except for our own personal stories as well as stories about known personalities, the names associated with other stories, where appropriate, have been changed to honor privacy and confidentiality.

Finally, Jean and Lee especially want to thank Bev for keeping the vision of this book alive and for bringing it to fruition.

Appreciating the Wisdom of Different Voices

Men's Voices:

Different Voices

Authors' Note

We hope that this book will be a wake-up call!

The birthing of your WomanSoul is a crucial delivery. Bringing yourSelf to life has far-reaching implications both personally and professionally. What brings you to life will enliven and enspirit others as well.

Our hope in writing this book is that it will facilitate personal exploration of your journey toward spiritual wholeness. We invite you to find your own path through the book as part of your personal journey of birthing WomanSoul. You may wish to pause and ponder, and even jot down a note or two (there's even enough space to write in the margins if you like). You may express your own feelings and thoughts at the end of each chapter, where you will find *Highlights* and *Personal Reflections* with questions and activities to help you. Or you might find it helpful to start a special journal where you can record your thoughts, hopes and concerns. On the other hand, you may wish simply to enjoy reading the book.

Although the material in this book is designed to be worked with on your own, it can often be helpful to work in a small-group setting. The *Highlights* and *Personal Reflections* sections can be a focal point for the group sessions. Discussing these issues with others can give you the support and accountability needed to make changes in all aspects of your life.

Resolve (in the first draft, this word was accidentally typed as *reloves* which on reflection may be an important new perspective on the word *resolve*) that in this new century you will begin to choose what brings you to life!

Jean, Bev and Lee

This is a book for women of all ages.

This is a book for women who want to learn about SoulPlay, about dance, touch, prayer and about SoulShimmer.

This is a book about connections—to self, God and others.

This is a book about Hope, about lifting up and enlivening the spirit.

This is a book about Healing and about Coming to Life.

This book is about fireworks and Ferris wheels, popcorn and pink cotton candy.

This book is about love and labor, prayer and passion.

Prologue

*The most compelling
beauty emerges from the
depth and texture of a
person's life and spirit.*
–Kathleen Fischer

When meeting women while doing research for this book, we asked many of them the question, "What brings you to life?" And, though we were intrigued by their answers, we were, even more so, excited by their delight in being asked. They were pleased that someone cared to help them find and put a name to the innermost yearnings of their heart, what is precious to their very soul.

Something wonderful happened in the weeks that followed this initial meeting as we found that the women came back to us and said such things as: "I am lifted up just thinking about what is special to me"; "I'm taking better care of myself and not feeling guilty about it, and my family and friends seem to appreciate me more now"; and "Can I add something important to my list?"

Here are some of their answers prompted by the question, "What brings you to life?"

"Being able to use my creative gifts"
"Music of many types"
"Meeting new people"
"Being in nature: the sights, sounds and scents"
"Watching children play...and playing with them"

---

 yourSelf: the crucial person you must care for, the one who needs nurturing and nourishment, space and time before you can help others or release your own creativity and passion for life.

What brings YOU to life?

This book is designed to help Bring You (yourSelf) to Life!

Your trueSelf has been very elusive, so secret that you may not even know of it, let alone really know it. However, you have had glimpses of your trueSelf through your innermost yearnings, but you have ignored or pushed them away as you strived to care for the needs of others in your life. You must find and allow the soul of your trueSelf to come forth. As you explore your trueSelf with the help of this book, you will release your own creativity and passion for life. In the process of becoming a creature fully alive, your connection to all of life will expand.

> *There are only two ways to live. One is as though nothing is a miracle. The other is as if everything is.*
>
> –Albert Einstein

Whether you are learning to connect with your trueSelf or how to deepen your connection with others and with God, you will become more in tune with the rhythms of the universe. As you discover your dance of life, you will find more space to relax, more freedom to move at your own pace and more time for creative ideas and feelings to penetrate your heart and soul.

We will also look at what women say deadens them and how you can find those areas in your own life that keep you from finding and actualizing your trueSelf.

We will engage you in many pathways as you come to appreciate the sacredness of your spirit, the essence of your trueSelf. One of our favorite pathways will be play and whimsy. Let yourSelf relax and be disarmed by the humor within and all around you. You will flow with greater flexibility in your new dance. Join the adventure as you find your unique and special gifts and, at the same time, be heartened to find other women whose soul resonates with yours. This is WomanSoul: the spirit within reaching out in connection to others and God and, yet, having space for ourselves and the freedom to get in touch with our trueSelves.

Are you intrigued to discover what brings women to Life, what touches their WomanSoul? Most importantly, do you wish to find and name your own life-giving essence? Do you desire to heal the hurts to your trueSelf and move away from the path that deadens you? There is hope in these pages. The pathways that bring you to Life lie ahead.

What Brings You to Life?

"Breathing, taking in every breath fully"

"Painting; making love"

"Beautiful music: hearing and feeling it; soothing, bouncy"

"Dancing, reading...everything!"

"A relaxing massage"

"Good warm weather, ocean waves and tropical breezes"

"Beautiful sunrises, sunsets"

"Water flowing over rocks"

"Fascinating patterns and textures"

"Spending time with family, both old and new, sharing new experiences, old stories; learning about each other"

"Synchronicity"

"Being able to choose what to do with my time, such as playing tennis"

"Rhythmic movement with kinesthetic awareness and balance"

"Swimming, exercises, walking"

"Nature, learning, art, dance, singing"

"Seasons' ebb and flow"

"Rocking babies"

1

Dancing to the Rhythms of Life

I'm tired, Lord,
but I'll lift one foot
if you'll lift the other for me.
–Saidie Patterson

There are so many ways to dance, so many ways to come to life! You can give yourself time and space to reflect quietly and tune in to the beat of your own drummer, or exercise to tone down with rhythmic movement that brings increasing flexibility. You can be a part of the dance of nature just by appreciating its many rhythms.

> *Dance is the divine expression*
> *of the human soul.*
> –Isadora Duncan

JEAN'S STORY: *Tree Dance*

I sit on my deck in the backyard and watch the old trees on the days when they dance, when they move in rhythm to the breezes with the leaves rustling in eager accompaniment. The swaying branches remind me (and us as well) that I can't dance when I am stiff and rigid. Regardless of your physical capabilities, you must be flexible in your mind and soul.

...What is your dance of life?

We begin to dance before we are born as we move to the rhythms of our mother's heartbeat and are swayed and rocked as she herself moves. It is no coincidence that more and more people every year are being drawn to beaches (40 percent of U.S. Americans in the late nineties, according to Stanley Plog). There, our bodies remember floating in wave-like motions within the womb and our senses hear again the roaring pulselike sounds coming through the placenta. The ocean's movement and sound are thrilling, yet at the same time its rhythmic ebb and flow are profoundly comforting, giving us a sense of security and timelessness.

LYNNE'S STORY: *Wave Dance*

Lynne's mother was afraid of the water, so her family didn't go to the beach. Her mother insisted that Lynne learn to swim for her own safety, but it was in a structured way and only in swimming pools. Twenty years passed before Lynne insisted to her husband (who is not really a beach person) that she needed to experience the wonder of the beach and the ocean. One summer, they were there only for a few days, but Lynne bought an inner tube with handles, thinking it would be wonderful just to feel the movement of the waves. So, they both held on to it, flowing with the waves. They both felt so relaxed, yet rejuvenated at the same time, being part of the rhythm of the wave dance. They both felt like kids, though they weren't playing and splashing in the waves, but simply feeling the need to be a part of the movement. At other times, Lynne had sat on the beach and watched the waves and the birds, took long walks and splashed at the water's edge, but, oh the life-giving beauty of feeling the movement in the waves.

A PEOPLE STORY: *More Fun If by Sea*

People are drawn to the water in other ways as well. Not long ago, in Annapolis, the capital of Maryland, work was being done to restore the Spa Creek Bridge. This is a small, old drawbridge that, when raised, allows sailboats to pass through. Though Annapolis is a lovely quaint town, it is considered the sailing capital of the world, so the drawbridge is rather important. In the closed position, it is the only direct route by car to downtown Annapolis from Eastport. However, during the restoration the bridge was closed to vehicular traffic. The people in Eastport referred to this cutoff as seceding from Annapolis. For several weeks, the only direct way that the people in Eastport could get to Annapolis was by water. The Annapolis Water Taxi began running more frequently, even though it usually didn't do so in winter because the boat is not only small but also has only one deck that is quite open to the elements. Even after the bridge had been restored, people asked to keep the Water Taxi available because they enjoyed being out on the water, hearing the natural sound of the waves and feeling the movement—as opposed to the mechanical movement of the cars going across the bridge.

We are fascinated by water, movement and the rhythms of the earth,

> *The best and most beautiful things in the world cannot be seen or even touched. They must be felt with the heart.*
>
> —Helen Keller

the cycles of life, the amazing ways of Mother Nature. It is no accident that nature is called Mother. The cycles of life and the ways of nature are especially apparent in the life cycles of the feminine gender.

LEE'S STORY: *Sex and Ice Cream*

When I was about eleven years old, I learned about the "facts of life" from a few friends who had gotten it all wrong and managed to utterly confuse me. I went to my mother, asking her if what I had heard could really be true—was life really like that? And, my mother matter-of-factly said, "You're talking about sex. It's not a hurtful thing; it's a good thing." In my wildest imagination, I could not fathom how what happened between men and women could possibly feel good, but my mother kept saying, "It's not to worry about; it's something you'll do when you're older. It's a good thing."

Still, that was not enough of an explanation; I had nothing to which I could relate it. It seemed incredibly strange. What did it feel like? How could it possibly be good? I said, "Is it good like ice cream?" "Yes, Lee," she said, "sex is good like ice cream." Then, I understood, and I trusted life again.

Even though this is a delightfully funny story, it is also a beautiful example of the trust that a young girl has for her mother. Not only can she bring her most profound questions to her mother, but her mother doesn't flinch or try to hedge when answering the "sex" question. She is very matter-of-fact with her daughter and doesn't try to frighten her further. The fact that Lee was able to trust life again after this reassurance says volumes about the importance of daughters being able to trust their mothers and the responsibility of mothers to give voice to their own values in the dance of life.

Humans have been dancing to universal rhythms since the beginning of time and dance is sacred to many traditional peoples, even today. In the Middle Ages, the processionals into the church included the *tripudium* step, a definite pattern of three steps forward and one step back. It could even be considered as a walking meditation.

> *You dance love,*
> *you dance joy*
> *And*
> *You dance dreams.*
> —Gene Kelly

Joseph Campbell spoke to a Shinto priest in Japan and asked about his ideology and theology. The priest said, "We don't have ideology; we don't have theology; we dance."

However, many religions fear that dancing, especially between the sexes, will corrupt the body and mind and detract from the spiritual aspects of their faith.

In some branches of Orthodox Judaism, men and women don't dance together. And, it is even joked about among Jews themselves that sex is not OK if it leads to dancing; dancing is the danger.

In contrast, some other conservative religious groups don't believe in dancing, partly because dancing could lead to frivolity or sex. Here we see different religious traditions concerned with the power of a life force to corrupt.

However, in the movie *The Next Karate Kid,* Mr. Miyagi proclaims, "Never trust spiritual leader who cannot dance."

Movies have the power to teach us many things about spirituality and dance bringing us to life. In Hasidim, a Jewish sect, as portrayed in the movie *Yentl,* the men will dance, as Greek men do, together, in a circle dance. In *Zorba the Greek,* Zorba was always trying to get his boss to dance.

Zorba was alive and he expressed himself in the dance. He danced when he was happy and he danced when he was sad, when his child died. But, he couldn't get his boss to dance. Finally, at the end of the movie, his boss did dance and with this movement, he came to life!

When Do Women Get to Dance?

Matthew Fox speaks of dancing Sarah's circle, a weaving in and out of our brothers' and sisters' lives as in folk dancing. Sarah, the wife of Abraham, was surprised and amazed when she conceived at the age of ninety (Gen 18:9-15). There was much rejoicing when she gave birth to Isaac (Gen 21:1-8). Fox is speaking of Sarah's circle as representing women connecting on a horizontal plane, in their work as well as in their dance. Women connect again and again as hands reach forth in welcome to grasp one person's hand and then another's. The patterns and motifs of these movements unfold in surprising beauty and mystic union with the joys and rhythms of the earth. Often, the spirit

> *...recreation as important*
> *As meditation:*
> *music and dance.*
> —St. Teresa of Avila

of our Creator can be found in the midst of the joy in celebration as well as in the compassion and connection of neighbor helping neighbor during difficult times.

All the seasons of a woman's life express what we are, and being faithful to what we are is essential in keeping us on the path of WomanSoul. What deadens us is being what we are not.

What deadens you?
"Not being given a choice"
"When my freedom is taken away and I can't move"
"Too much structure"
"Fear that closes me up; mud-stickin' fears"
"I hate being inactive, but I have no choice due to my illness"

"Constraints that are unnecessary"

"Overexertion and fatigue, decreased sleep"

"Getting up early; I really don't do mornings well"

As we listen to some of what deadens women, we hear that constraint of movement is a recurring theme. Over the centuries, women have been told what to say, how to dress and how to act. Even more menacing to women's spirits is being told how to think and even how to feel. Couple these constraints with the many commitments of women's time, only some of which we have freely chosen, and the resultant fatigue may seem unending.

Who constrains us? In some cases we constrain ourselves by doing what women are "supposed" to do. We have been used to being defined rather than defining ourselves. We have been trained to listen to social constraints and, therefore, our trueSelves are hidden, even from ourselves. Therefore, we don't always know what we *really* want to do. In some cases, we feel we have no choice, such as when we are the most "logical" choice to have the care of an elderly parent or parent-in-law. Though it can be rewarding and meaningful, those women who do not have help in this caregiving can be under considerable strain.

In other cases, women increasingly have to decide between whether they want a career or a home and family. Or, if we try to manage both, we end up with even less freedom. We have little enough quality time with our family and no time and space for our own self-care. When the men in our lives share the work and care of the home and family, women not only appreciate it but discover that there is more time to develop that adult relationship, as well.

But all too often, men not only don't help but may hinder. They may even be the cause of major constraints on women's time and space. Even beyond the personal level, men often have dictated women's career paths, fashion trends, the medical care given to women and even what type of health research is appropriate for women. It seems as if men feel they know women better than the women know themselves and, therefore, the men know what is best for women. It appears also that men perhaps have a need to feel superior—and that may necessitate, in their minds, control over women's lives.

Menacing Menses

The author and humorist Barbara Johnson titled one of her chapters, "MENacing MENstrual Cramps, MENopause, MENtal Failure... Is There a Connection Here?" Even if men have had a great deal of influence over women's lives, we can't, of course, blame men for all of our ills.

The way I see it, if you want the rainbow, you gotta put up with the rain.

—Dolly Parton

Certainly women's cycles and especially menstruation have an important purpose, but the accompanying cramps serve only to cramp our style (no pun intended). They can be quite severe and debilitating as can a heavy menstrual flow that can leave girls and women quite anemic. Many of us who are over age fifty were given very little information about our menstrual cycles when we were growing up. Unlike Lee's mother, most of our mothers couldn't or wouldn't talk to us about such things, and this accounted for much whispering among our girlfriends at school and knowing looks from the older girls. Sometimes, we would be given a girls' health pamphlet to read or a movie to watch at school about how wonderful it was that our bodies were changing in a special way. The fact that boys were not allowed to see the movie made it all the more mysterious for us, not to mention that it made the boys absolutely determined to uncover this deep secret. By this time, many of the girls felt completely humiliated, and when one of us did have her first "period" she was often panicked about what to do and how to care for herself. Heaven forbid if she had an "accident" and no sanitary "protection" with her and no warning that her "period" was starting. This was the ultimate embarrassment! A close second was buying sanitary pads, which in the fifties were in boxes that were wrapped in plain brown paper—no, we're not fooling! Notice the term "period," which is one of only several euphemisms used for menstruation. A few of the many others include, "cycle," "the curse," "the plague," "came on," "monthlies," "flow," "on the rag" and "falling off the roof." We kid you not, especially about that last phrase; read Lee's story.

LEE'S STORY: *Falling off the Roof and Other Secret Codes My Mother Used*

One day when I was a child I overheard my mother talking on the tele-phone to her sister, something she did every day, but this time I heard her say something that terrified me. She told her sister that she fell off the roof yesterday. I could not understand why my mother did not tell me that she fell off the roof. It seemed a monumental event. I couldn't understand how she survived, and yet I didn't see any bruises; I didn't see any sign that she had been hurt at all. She had simply said that she wasn't feeling very well that day, that she had fallen off the roof. I wanted to ask my mother about when she had fallen off the roof and how far she fell and where it really hurt her and, in fact, whether she had broken any bones. But nothing seemed to be broken, and I went off to play, and falling off the roof receded to somewhere in the more remote parts of my memory.

It was not until forty years later, while we authors were discussing how women referred to their menstrual cycles, that I heard somebody say that her mother had fallen off the roof, and I began to realize that falling off the roof had more than a literal meaning. At that moment, time fell away for me and I could hear again, so plainly, my mother speaking to her sister. To this day, I have no idea what falling off the roof has to do with menstruation. It was just one of those secret codes that my mother and many other mothers used to communicate something very special about being a woman.

Though women's cyclical functions are very special, they are also the source of much controversy around the world. Many taboos have developed, some perpetuated by men, to keep women apart from society when they are menstruating, or at least to forbid them to touch revered objects, lest they spoil them.

In many parts of the world, women who are menstruating are considered "unclean" during that time, as well as for several weeks after giving birth—when small amounts of blood continue until the uterus completely heals. Women are often housed separately during these times. In addition, signs are placed outside of some temple entrances, forbidding menstruating women to enter. In people's homes, objects such as ivory are not to be touched when a woman is "bleeding" because it is believed that the object may darken in color at that site and be considered ruined.

Are women forbidden to participate when menstruating as an excuse to exclude them, or is there some fear of this bodily flow and the power thought to be behind it? It is probably some combination of the two, yet this is but one of many different types of exclusion of women found in all societies.

Though men may not envy a woman's bleeding times, it might also be that many men down through the centuries have been amazed at women's ability to bring forth new life. And, they have envied that miracle of creation, especially before it was known that men's "seed" helped to bring about that new creation. Perhaps "womb envy" is the reason many men have desired to keep women from succeeding in other realms, such as work and sports.

Surging Summer Moments

It would be very surprising if men were envious of "men-o-pause." Who would want the possibility of hot flashes and accompanying irritability, forgetfulness, depression and increased yet unpredictable uterine bleeding? There is also major sleep deprivation, especially related to the hot flashes in the middle of the night. You wake up sweltering, so you throw off the blankets, and then you get chilled and you pull the covers back on, and then you repeat the cycle many times in one night. Some women now refer to the hot flashes as "power surges," but "summer moments" is our (these authors') favorite phrase. In any case, it helps to reframe more positively that which can be very debilitating in women's lives.

It's hard to remember those cold winters of the past when more blankets helped us to sleep better, except for those winters during pregnancy when the blankets were peeled off at night due to our increased body heat. And, now, the heat's been turned up again, but this time unpredictably so that the "summer moments" are felt when we least expect them. And, wouldn't it be great if we got a dollar every time one of us said, "Is it hot in here, or is it me?"

As the reproductive cycles and rhythms within a woman's body begin to taper off, creating new life must come from within herSelf. Those seeds that penetrate must come from her soul, her WomanSoul.

 WomanSoul: the spirit within reaching out in connection to others and God and, yet, having space for ourselves and the freedom to get in touch with our trueSelves—our life-giving essence.

Dancing in High Heels (and Backwards No Less)

In order to allow that creative new life to blossom forth from within, we need balance in our life. We need to play as well as work, dance as well as meditate and gather loved ones to us as well as find oases of solitude. As women, we have done many things, tried to satisfy many people and expect to do even more in the future. We need to remind ourselves that we do have many abilities and we don't have to keep proving it to ourselves and others. Some years ago, Texas governor Ann Richards pointed out the irony that "while Fred Astaire received top billing, 'Ginger Rogers did everything that Fred Astaire did. She just did it backwards and in high heels.'" This comment illustrates not only our abilities, but also our flexibility in mind and movement.

> *Dance is for everyone.*
> *It kindles the human spirit*
> *and encourages creativity.*
>
> —Buffa Hargett

But, therein is the real irony. If our minds are so flexible, why do we find ourselves still stuck in high heels as the ideal in feminine footwear? Those ideals come from men's points of view, and we have bought them—in more ways than one. If high heels are so great, then why aren't men still wearing them (no offense to cowboys)?

Erma Bombeck loved to poke fun at women's not-so-helpful fashions, and high heels were a favorite issue of hers. She felt that we should not only not wear them, but never donate them to needy people, who really don't need them.

On the more serious side, foot fashions are maiming us if not actually killing us, though most women have said at some time, "My feet are killing me!" In a survey done by the American Orthopaedic Foot and Ankle Society (we don't make these names up), it was found that eight out of ten women said that their shoes were painful to wear. Susan Okie stated that with a three-and-one-quarter-inch heel, there is ten times greater pressure on the forefoot than if the person wore flat shoes. We don't need more pressure; we need the freedom to dance to the rhythms all around us. So...*Keep those feet happy...You can't dance unless you have happy feet!*

If God helps those who help themselves, then God probably would find it easier to help us keep our balance or to lift the other foot for us when we are tired, if we weren't wobbling on high heels.

Enough references to high heels! We had better stop before someone starts throwing some at us.

If you were free to move to the universal rhythms of swaying branches, lilting birdsong, babbling brooks and the canter of horses hooves, would you be ready and eager to do so?

I wanted a perfect ending...
Now I've learned, the hard way,
that some poems don't rhyme,
and some stories don't have a clear
beginning, middle, and end. Life is
about not knowing, having to change,
taking the moment and making the
best of it, without knowing what's
going to happen next.

—Gilda Radner

In a few years, will you look back and say,

"If only..."

or

"What if..."?

Dare to dance the song that comes from your trueSelf!

19

HIGHLIGHTS

Your world can come alive, if you bring yourSelf to Life...

Appreciate circles and cycles and mystic union...

Find your own rhythm; follow your own path...

Trust your trueSelf...

Enjoy secret codes and mysterious happenings...

Yearn to succeed in being wholly yourSelf...

Find what would allow you to dance with meaning...

Discover where you are hiding your wings...

Find what lifts your spirit and let it soar...

Blossom forth from within...

Remember your blessings, even the little ones...

Open your life to the poetry in your soul...

Come dance with God...

PERSONAL REFLECTIONS

1. What brings you to life?

2. What deadens you?

3. In this chapter, we speak about dancing to the rhythm of life. What is your "dance of life" and how do you express it?

4. How or when do you feel most constrained in your life?

5. What would help you get "unstuck"?

6. Can you free yourself, or do you need some help? Name a friend or professional who could give you that needed push or pull to help free you.

7. What messages did you receive from your mother or other significant female figures about what it means to be a woman? What were the messages sent about women's bodily changes, such as menstruation, pregnancy and menopause? How are these messages affecting you now? Positively? Negatively? Are there some different messages that you want to substitute for some of your childhood ones?

8. We spoke about women and fashion. Are there fashions that you personally don't like but are afraid not to wear? Are you dressing for yourSelf, or for comfort, or to "fit in," or to impress others? Just think about these questions, recognizing you don't have to change your behavior unless you choose to.

9. Are there some "If Onlys. . ." and "What Ifs... " that you are experiencing now? Explore them. What do they have to teach you about how you are opening to or deadening the song of life within yourSelf?

What Brings You to Life?

"Being with loved ones and sharing special family moments"

"Planning a future of dreams and hopes with a loving man"

"Hugs from my kids"; "playing and reading with grandchildren"

"Being with others who enjoy children and are excited by what they are doing"; "seeing people enjoy each other"

"Seeing my grown children being successful in many areas of their lives"

"A renewed connection with my mother—the new understanding and communication we now share and hope to share for the rest of our lives"

"Spending time with my husband; the real presence of a person"

"Time spent with good friends"; "knowing I am loved"

"God"; "A feeling that I'm not alone, God is with me"

"Anything created by God: light, plants, animals"; "beauty of nature"; "being outside: being able to see it, be a part of it, taste it"

"Being needed; working and sharing with interesting people"

"Being able to help others; serving others with joy"

"Connecting with myself: losing weight; having a massage"

"Having good communication with others"; "good discussions"

What Brings You to Life?

"Receiving affirmation"; "an encouraging word or compliment"

"Spending time with Chloe"

"Appreciating beauty in many forms of art"

2

Connection Is Everything

Blessed is the influence of one true,
loving human soul on another.
—George Eliot (Marian Evans)

We were born connected!

And, then...our lifeline was cut. Our first major disconnection leaves us gasping, not only for breath but for the warmth and security of the chamber that enclosed, rocked and protected us. We were blinded by the first light, chilled by the air moving past us and foiled in our attempts to contain our flailing limbs. Our hands grasped for dear life at the first touch to our palms.

Beyond that moment of birth, we strive our whole lives to find the proper balance between security and adventure that will nourish and enrich us. If we are fortunate to have a loving home with caring people, we will know the security and trust that will allow us to develop into the unique individuals we were meant to be, while reaching out in caring connection to others.

> *The infant's experience, at birth: A blooming, buzzing confusion.*
>
> —William James

lifeSpirit: moving forth in freedom and adventure or peaceful contemplation, from a grounding of ·trust, support and security.

In many different ways, connecting in all aspects of our lives gives us the necessary support to step forth and use our own unique gifts in creative ways. Connecting with others enlivens our lifeSpirit to become an integral part of our WomanSoul.

A MOTHER'S STORY: *The Big Booming Voice*

When her daughter, Sara, was being treated for leukemia, Carol Kruckeberg asked their minister, Elmer, where was "the big booming voice from above? Why haven't we heard from God? Why?" The minister asked her what held her together and kept her on her feet? Carol replied, "The phone calls. The letters. Our family. Our friends. They shoulder in close. Sometimes they lift us above it all."

Then Elmer said, "Maybe there's your big, booming voice."

Most women have told us that what brings them to life is connecting with others, including God and God's creations. Many women spoke of working and sharing with others, and being in and appreciating nature. True connection with others and God cannot be fully appreciated unless there is a connection with the Self as well. A few women spoke of being able to experience connection that would enhance themselves personally in physical, spiritual and emotional ways. Whether it is in caring for our bodies through good food (especially food that is good for us–including chocolate, of course) and relaxing massages or accepting an encouraging word or special affirmation, it is essential that we care for the precious Self that God has given us. We dare not squander our energy or refuse to develop our creative gifts.

The connection with the trueSelf is really liking what we find inside, just as a friend would appreciate us. Eleanor Roosevelt said, "Friendship with oneself is all-important because without it one cannot be friends with anyone else in the world." Similarly, Abraham Lincoln stated, "I desire so to conduct the affairs of this administration that if at the end, when I come to lay down the reins of power, I have lost every other friend on earth, I shall at least have one friend left, and that friend shall be down inside of me."

What Do You Say after You Say, "Hello, Self"?

How do you develop a relationship or connection with yourSelf in order to have that friendship that both Eleanor Roosevelt and Abraham Lincoln considered to be so essential? Perhaps it is similar to developing a relationship with oth-

> It is wise to begin small, take root, and then grow.
> —Mary Breckenridge

ers. We guess you have to meet yourSelf and say, "Hello, Self." The further question is what do you say after you say "Hello"? Perhaps you could say, "What brings you to life?" Or you could write a special letter of appreciation to yourSelf on very nice stationery. On the other hand, perhaps you don't think yourSelf deserves this special treatment, or that it may seem silly, or self-indulgent. You may wish to consider your reasons for that reaction.

Additionally, if you've been abused in some way in your life, you may not even be able to say "Hello." You may not think you have value, and you may be afraid to know about yourSelf because you may have assumed the blame for the abuse. There may be judgmental and critical phrases being replayed inside of you. It is not unusual for us to say negative things to ourselves at times. We need to learn to counter those sayings and to encourage ourselves so that we may then be able to encourage others. But first we may need to get help for ourselves.

> *With true beauty this true self, like hidden precious treasure, awaits discovery and development.*
> —George Aschenbrenner

Many women guard against thinking of "self" first, and yet it has become even more necessary to do so in our modern world, where there is a vast complex of connections in many spheres of activities. In addition to the more classical spheres such as home, career, school, community and church, women are involved with the latest technologies, including the Internet. Our personal and professional connections form a stronger web than any international computer network. And yet these electronic networks clearly indicate our need for connections. People search for ways to throw the connection net wider and wider. We can be in touch with the whole world in seconds. On the other hand, the messages received and the forays into the Web can be very intrusive and time consuming, often leaving little time to be in touch with ourselves. For some, there is a real risk of making unhealthy, habit-forming, addictive connections. But even if you have the control to break contact with the simple press of a key when computer associations become too intense, you are often left with a sense of disconnection and isolation. Computer communication is often depersonalized. It can become merely a stream of words back and forth without the personal intimacy usually found in a handwritten note. This is precisely where that special note makes a difference again, now written from your trueSelf to someone you care about.

After you meet yourSelf, you are going to have to nurture yourSelf. Whether stretched out reading a good book while listening to ocean waves or birdsong, or soaking in a hot and bubbly tub bath with your favorite music playing while surrounded by scented candles, this is your special time. Whatever is specific to your own needs, you are hanging out with yourSelf. (For more ways to nurture yourSelf, see chapter 4: The Wonder of Space and Time: A Gift to Womanhood.)

JEAN'S STORY: *Re-treat YourSelf*

For the past fifteen years, I've been going on retreat at least two times a year. I especially like to go on three-to-five-day silent retreats. The idea of not talking can seem frightening to many people, and I guess that I felt that way the first time, too. People sometimes say to me, "What's it like when you stop talking?" Actually, what happens for me when I stop talking is that I become more aware of the continual dialogue that is going on inside me. Quieting down that inner chatter is actually more difficult for me than not talking out loud to others.

Why do I go on silent retreats? It gives me time to stop the often frantic pace of life. The first time that I'd had an extended time of silence, I was so surprised to discover this deep place of stillness within me. It felt like coming home to my center. I call this still place my Higher Self or the God within. Taking extended periods of silence helps me more easily reconnect with that still place during my daily meditation times.

I don't want to give the impression that it's always just "sweetness and light" when I am on a silent retreat. Issues come up when I am quiet. I think that's part of why we all race around so much. We don't want to face some of the inner demons lurking within us. But I've learned that there is a gift in facing my demons. Naming them seems to give them less power in my life and ultimately gives me more freedom.

What do I do on a silent retreat? I read, I walk, I draw, I listen to music, I pray, I meditate and I sleep. The first time that I went on a silent retreat I was really shocked at how tired I was. Living on the "adrenaline high" of our modern life can mask the deep, deep tiredness within. Time seems to slow down on retreat. It's hard to explain. I don't mean time drags. Actually, time seems to expand. I find myself moving more slowly and eating more slowly. I am truly more aware of life and living.

Silent retreats help me to connect deeply to my Self, to the world around me and especially to God.

We as women make time for all sorts of other people and demands in our lives. Silent retreats can give us the space and time that we need for rejuvenation. Likewise, on a retreat we can connect with others whom we trust and still find the needed space and time to be alone.

> *Be still, and know that I am God.*
>
> —Psalm 46:10
>
> *God abides in us and his love is perfected in us.*
>
> —1 John 4:12

JEAN'S STORY: *Beach Women Friends with Assorted Fans and Blankets*

Since 1981, I've been spending a week at the beach with twelve women. We started doing this when we were all divorced single parents and our beach week was the only time when we weren't responsible for anyone but ourselves. We used to say that this is our time with no men and no kids.

It's interesting to think about how this beach week has evolved over the years. For the first several years, our beach house was a rundown place with no air conditioning (AC) and a long walk to the beach. It was all that we could afford then. For the past nine years we've been renting a lovely seven-bedroom, five-bathroom house right on the ocean. Originally our conversations were about dating and raising kids. Lately we've been talking about aging, menopause and grandchildren.

Connection Is Everything

Although we were all divorced when we started, most of us have remarried. I remember telling my soon-to-be husband many years ago, "You have to understand that one week each summer I need to go away and be with my beach women friends." Fortunately, he understood.

Over the years we've developed some practices that make our week together work for us. We are all on our own for breakfast and lunch. We usually pair up and take turns being "house parents" for a day. That means that one day out of seven, two of us are responsible for planning the menu, doing the grocery shopping, cooking dinner and cleaning up. We actually have some fabulous meals. When faced with having to cook only one meal in the week, we've discovered

> *Slowly, and slower, you have learned to let yourselves grow strong while weaving through each other in strong cloth....*
>
> —Marge Piercy

how much fun it is to be very creative. We've also learned to give one another the space we need. Actually, there is a lot of freedom in the fact that there are so many of us. No one feels obligated to have to always be "good company." I often go for a long walk by myself or sit alone in my room journaling or napping, or I put my chair in a quiet corner of the deck and read for hours. There is such freedom in having a lot of time to be with people you care about but also in having enough time to be alone as well.

People sometimes ask me, "How can twelve women be together in one house? Don't you get on one another's nerves?" I answer, "Yes, sometimes we do." Our latest little hassles have been about the temperature in the house. Some of us like the AC turned down low to help combat hot flashes. Others don't like the AC at all. We laugh about coming to the beach with our assorted fans and blankets. The reality is that we now have a long history with one another and we've learned to work through problems together. We trust one another and know that this is a time when it is safe to be "real." However, we all agree that the main reason we've been able to sustain this long commitment is because we meditate together each morning. This spiritual bond and connection has helped sustain us through some trying times of health problems, relationship problems and personality conflicts.

This is a very nurturing time for each of us. We laugh a lot. Some nights we stay up late, eat popcorn, and giggle like a bunch of girls at a slumber party. Other nights everyone's tired and we go to bed at 9 P.M. For years we've been keeping a beach journal filled with priceless quotes like "What does hunger have to do with eating?" and "Fat tastes good." We are very different people. A few of these women are my closest friends, while some I rarely see from one beach week till the next. Somehow it all works out.

When we started going to the beach together, we never said that we were going to do this forever. It just sort of evolved. Now there is serious commitment to this time together. We all lead active, busy lives and to keep this one-week commitment for so many years demonstrates how important this is for us. It is a healing, nurturing time. We talk about what will happen when one of us dies or is too ill to come to the beach, and we know that we'll find ways to continue our commitment no matter what the future brings.

> *But friendship, like all things, needs time for ripening.*
> —Madeleine L'Engle

Giving ourselves time for retreats and for vacations with friends are ways of nurturing our body, mind and spirit. Unfortunately, some people think that taking time for yourSelf is the same as being selfish or lazy. As women, many of us have been taught to always put others' needs first and our own needs last. Connection with Self and learning the importance of self-nurturing is part of our task in the journey toward healing.

Most people were raised to share with others. As children, many of us were taught scripture verses that we were told emphasized thinking of others rather than ourselves, such as the second commandment: "You shall love your neighbor as yourself" (Mark 12:31). For many years this commandment was interpreted as caring for our neighbor at one's own sacrifice. Today, it is seen in a much different light. For if we do not take good care of ourselves, we will not have the strength and heart to care for others.

LEE'S STORY: *I Love You All, but I Can't Connect with Eighteen of You at Once*

For the past several years, I've been living alone, though I have four married children and, at the time this story took place, ten grandchildren. There were five girls and five boys ranging in age from two to fourteen.

On my birthday, they all came to visit me at once. It's true that they made dinner, and it's true that they cleaned up. Also true, however, is that somebody's wet trunks were found on the seat of my piano, a piano that I had just had refinished at considerable cost. "Of course, it was an accident," I said, gritting my teeth. So was the spillage on the newly recarpeted dining room floor.

These are material things; they can be taken care of. The real tragedy of the day was that I couldn't be with everybody in the family who wanted to be with me, and I couldn't communicate my frustration to them. I love them all, but eighteen at one time was a bit much.

At the end of the day, my children felt the party had been a failure. I overheard them talking to each other. "I wonder if she liked it?" one of them said. "I hardly saw her," another said. "Where was she when we called her for dinner?" said a third. The fact of the matter is, I had been with all of them, but only for a very short time with each.

Perhaps it will take some time to recognize that, though I love each of them, I can't communicate with all of them at once. Maybe this is the reason why there comes a certain time in a woman's life, when instead of everyone coming to mother's house, mother begins to visit each child's family separately. Love is one thing, but numbers can be overwhelming.

It can be fun to have the whole family together, but concentrating on the depth of each relationship is difficult with so much stimulation all at one time. Thus, when it comes to true connection, we often need to have space and time to regenerate our inner heartSelves, and then enough time to share that heartfelt love with those whose connections are important in our lives. Women have learned to network and to share responsibilities so that they might have that needed time and space.

There is a Chinese proverb that says, "Women hold up half the sky." In many parts of the world, women's burden of responsibility is often more than half, whether or not it is recognized. Even in the United States, where 15,769,000 women are heads of households (11.4 percent of the labor force) women have tremendous and frequently unappreciated responsibilities. Networking is a vital necessity to ease the burden of child care, continuing education, work schedules and providing a home. These are the practical, everyday concerns of most people. But, if women hold up their half of the sky in sharing the weight of responsibilities, so do they also enlighten us spiritually and bring peace to their communities near and far. Often, women are closer to the interrelatedness of all nature and therefore resonate with the grand design of the universe: the seasons and cycles, birth and growth, courage and hope.

The universe is itself a work of art, with God as the first Artist, the first Poet....

—Luci Shaw

Connection Is Everything

LEE'S STORY: *Nancy—A Portrait in Courage*

Nancy came to school in a wheelchair. A woman in her mid-thirties returning to college like many ambulatory women, Nancy came each week to the "Women's Program," a program that combined guidance and counseling with the course work.

One day, Nancy said, "You should establish a program similar to this for handicapped people." (In those days, the word handicapped *was used instead of* disabilities, *or as an adjective instead of the phrase "people with handicaps.") After some discussion, I said that I would try to obtain funding for such a program but that I couldn't run it. Nancy said, "I'll do it if you can get the college to support it."*

Almost miraculously, the administration of the college told me to go ahead and try such a program with a grant from the state's Department of Education. And so, Nancy and I put an ad in the local paper that simply said, "If you are handicapped and if you want to come to college, appear at such and such a place and time." Much to our surprise, more than twenty people showed up. Some were mentally challenged, several came in wheelchairs and others had physical and emotional disabilities that were equally dramatic but not equally visible. All of them, however, wanted to learn. I reconfirmed that I could not run such a program by myself. And Nancy restated, "I'll do it." I don't know where she got the energy or the strength, but she did it. Called Single Step, the first group started two businesses called the Handy Action Factions. In the first business, people made flies for fly fishing, and in the second, people went out to clean homes using a handicap-accessible van for transportation. All of the cleaners couldn't do all parts of the job, so each person did some of it, and they worked together to get the job done.

> Take the first step in faith. You don't have to see the whole staircase, just take the first step.
>
> —Martin Luther King, Jr.

Twenty-five years later, that program still exists. A recent reunion brought several hundred people back to Dundalk Community College in Maryland, where it all began with a single step. It began also with a single woman who refused to be limited mentally by her physical limitations and who believed that a dream could become a reality.

The difficulties that you have had in your life can make you a miserable person or, having had support and encouragement, you can move around difficulties as did Nancy.

Even with a wholesome childhood, none of us escapes problems as we move through life. We only can search for and hopefully find the spirit to rise above them.

LEE'S STORY: *I'm No Kid, but My Nose Knows*

If I give you
a rose,
you will not
doubt God.
—Clement of Alexandria

Recently, while in Portland, Oregon, I had the opportunity to visit the city's famous rose gardens. My three able-bodied friends offered to remain with me rather than climb the many terraces that I could not even attempt because of a back-pain problem that has limited my range of motion and my ability to climb steps. I sent my thoughtful companions forward, saying that I was content to sit on the ledge and view the gardens from there. Torn between caring for me and wanting to see it all, they finally went ahead after much prodding from me.

I sat on the ledge and noticed a child walking, even jumping on a ledge two terraces below. I remembered when I could jump like the child and wished I could do so now. But, the natural setting was so beautiful that I noticed the hundreds—no, thousands—of roses blooming on the level where I was sitting. I got up and decided to enjoy the beauty, not only with my eyes, but also with my nose—to smell the roses so near to me.

By the time my friends returned, I was familiar with the sight and smell of at least twenty different kinds of roses, and they were amazingly different! One, a velvety-looking large fuchsia-colored rose smelled so sweet that I knew I wanted my friends to enjoy its fragrance.

When they returned, they were eager to tell me of the many varieties of roses that they saw, as I led them toward the special rose that I had found. Upon inhaling the perfume, they asked me how I had connected with this one out of so many. "By moving from my childhood and connecting with my present age and condition," I replied. I could no longer walk and jump on ledges, yet there was an experience of a different sort that's perhaps finer, more delicate and even more precious.

> *...the radiance of the rose and the whiteness of the lily do not take away from the fragrance of the little violet or the delightful simplicity of the daisy.*
>
> —St. Thérèse of Lisieux

Here, then, is a connection with nature that bridges the past and the present with implications for future emotional and spiritual well-being, despite physical obstacles. The following story bridges another of our connections with nature in the present; one that spans our hope for the future, with implications of ancient instinct and wisdom.

BEV'S STORY: *Beach Scanner: Connecting to Animals Who Teach Us Amazing Lessons*

Some years ago, while walking along the shores of the Chesapeake Bay, I noticed a woman being very still and looking at something in the sand. I

> *The fullness of joy is to behold God in everything.*
>
> —Julian of Norwich

slowed my movements and then stopped completely when I realized it was a turtle laying her eggs. For a half hour, the turtle, supporting herself with only her front legs, alternated between digging with her back webbed feet and straining into the opening she had made. She would dig and strain, dig and strain, and occasionally her mouth would gape open, as if to cry out with the intense labor. Then, she spent five minutes carefully covering the eggs, moving slowly in a radial pattern and tamping down the sand with her back feet, smoothing it with the webbed part. Then, she looked all around, turned and headed directly to the water. Even then, she moved out only a short distance, looked around at the spot where the eggs were laid and moved out a bit farther from shore. She repeated this three to four times and then, finally, moved out farther into the bay. It was as if she wanted to be certain that the eggs containing her offspring, would be safe.

This wonderful act of nature would have been fascinating to most people but was even more absorbing to us two women—I, who had been a certified nurse-midwife, and the woman watching with me who was due to deliver her baby in less than a month. We did not know each other, but there was an immediate bond between us, a connection to nature and the necessary struggle of females to bring forth the young of the species.

The woman said that to some extent she had been afraid of her baby's forthcoming birth, but after witnessing this miracle, she better understood the need for the strain of labor. She considered herself very fortunate because she would not be alone during the process and would be able to see and hold her newborn after the long struggle.

But, the turtle story does not end here for me. I had found out that this had been a crucial turtle event of the diamondback terrapin, which is considered an endangered species. Though I was not around to see the little hatchlings, I did return to that spot exactly one year later and fondly remembered the turtle and the small but poignant drama in the *web of life. As I sat quietly, I noticed a turtle's head in the water near shore. It moved slowly back and forth and occasionally came close to the water's edge. If a gull or children came too near the shore, the turtle backed off farther into the water. This slow water dance continued for over two hours until she felt there was a safe space of time and place. I say she because I believed, after watching those first few cautious movements toward shore, that indeed it was a female turtle getting ready to lay her eggs.*

You can imagine that I remained very still during this whole time, except to ask the children not to go too close, but they moved off and the gull did also. The turtle then went through the half-hour process of digging and straining and then covering the eggs just like the year before. She moved to the water and did her checking several times before moving off, just as I remembered the turtle doing the previous year. Do you wonder, as I did, whether this was the same turtle? It was on the same day at approximately the same time, and it definitely was the same spot. I am still amazed, but I no longer wonder.

Connections of many types can bring you to life. Whether you are marveling at the wonders of nature, enjoying the company of family and friends or spending quiet time in relaxation and meditation, allow yourSelf to be nurtured. Appreciate who you are becoming.

Your life can make a difference! Reaching out through connections to others stretches your own heart and soul and fashions the world around you into a better place for all of us to dwell.

HIGHLIGHTS

Nourish yourSelf...

Give yourSelf permission...

Use your own unique gifts in creative ways...

Enliven your lifeSpirit: connect to God, Self and others...

Collect affirmations...

Enjoy more chocolate and massages...

Listen to the ocean waves and birdsong...

Let a puppy nuzzle your neck...

Slow the frantic pace...

Rise above your difficulties with support and encouragement...

Laugh at assorted fans and blankets...

Enjoy the precious flowers near you...

Learn from the creatures who are in tune with nature...

Appreciate who you are becoming...

Build bridges; sow seeds...

Give birth to yourSelf...

PERSONAL REFLECTIONS

1. Find your own balance between security and adventure. As you look at the following scale, where do you find yourself living most of your life?

←————————————————————————————————→

    Security   Balance   Adventure

List some areas of security in your life, some areas of adventure, and some areas of balance. Compare the lists. Are there any places in which you want to make some changes?

2. In this chapter, we use quotes from Eleanor Roosevelt and Abraham Lincoln, telling us that having a friendship with ourselves is essential. Do you agree with this? Do you have a friendship with yourSelf? How do you meet yourSelf? How can you develop a deeper relationship with yourSelf?

3. Regularly keeping a journal can often be a way for a woman to learn to *listen* to her own voice. Remember, a journal isn't a diary of daily activities. Instead it is a place in which you can be honest with yourSelf about what you think and feel. Explore your creativity within your journal. It's not just a place for writing—you can also draw in your journal, or paste in pictures or quotes from other sources. Try keeping a journal for two

months and see if it helps you to learn to listen more clearly to yourSelf. Sometimes rereading your old journals can help you discover your true voice.

4. Often women experience confusion between the words *selfish* and *self-care*. In your own words, define *selfish*. Define *self-care* or *self-nurturing*.

5. Below are twenty ideas for self-nurturing. Highlight one or two that you already do. You might want to add some others that are special for you. Pick one of these self-nurturing ideas and make a promise to yourself to do it *this week*! Try to do at least one self-nurturing activity a week.

   1. Take a warm bubble bath.
   2. Have breakfast in bed.
   3. Get a massage or manicure.
   4. Buy yourself a favorite flower.
   5. Take a walk. Look and listen to nature.
   6. Wake up early and watch the sunrise.
   7. Relax with a good book.
   8. Listen to your favorite music.
   9. Rent a funny video.
   10. Fix a special dinner just for yourself and eat by candlelight.
   11. Take a nap.
   12. Buy yourself a stuffed animal and hug it.
   13. Play with clay, paint, colored pencils or crayons.
   14. Write yourself a love letter and mail it.

15. Let yourself sit quietly and just BE without having to DO anything.
16. Sit in a church or synagogue.
17. Bake or cook something special.
18. Play with a child.
19. Go to the library and get books/tapes that interest you.
20. Pet an animal.
21.
22.
23.
24.

6. What are some important areas of connection for you? It might be nature, animals, people, places, spiritual beings or others. What fosters connection for you? How do you balance your need for connections to others with your need for connections to yourSelf?

What Brings You to Life?

"*Everything around me that makes me laugh, hope, feel, see, listen, give and know love*"

"*Feeling that my life has meaning; I'm making a contribution*"

"*Freedom in worship*"

"*Beautiful environment; sounds of birds*"

"*The sweet scent of a baby*"

"*Living, enjoying, being present in the moment*"

"*Great books and music; a nice walk; tea in china cups*"

"*Sewing, arts and crafts*"

"*Beautiful etched crystal in vibrant colors*"

"*Enjoying something with a passion: the beauty of nature, good food, flavored coffee, appreciating good-looking men*"

"*Accomplishing something; volunteering with the Scouts*"

"*A challenge: physical or mental*"

"*Synthesizing ideas and writing the results*"

"*Working with a group toward a goal*"

"*Fallow time*"

"*Beautiful clothes*"

"*Affirmation; sense of goodness in people*"

"*Joy on people's faces when I visit them: clown in hospital*"

"*Following my heart*"

3

Valuing Your True Essence along the Journey

If you travel far enough,
one day you will recognize yourself
coming down the road to meet you.
And you will say YES.
—Marion Woodman

When you follow your heart, you find your true values. Seek the essence of what you value and your life will have joy and meaning. Your trueSelf will bring you to life!

---

 trueSelf: the sacredness of your spirit, the essence of who you really are—often hidden from your own knowledge and understanding, but sometimes glimpsed through your inner-most yearnings and values.

Tuning in and Turning on to Your Values

Values define the importance of what's real and what is cherished, what "turns you on." We have values in many aspects of our lives as can

> *When you're dealing with music, you're dealing with the soul of society.*
>
> —Itzhak Perlman

be seen by what brings us to life and gives our lives meaning, whether in leisure, work, being with others or in quiet times of reflection. By connecting with these values, we can learn to appreciate and develop our gifts and talents as well as those of others which can have benefit for all of us.

SALLY'S STORY: *Haunting Melodies*

Sally awoke to a delightful spring morning. And, though she was uplifted by the sun and gentle breeze, Sally realized that she had a big decision to make. A friend had called to say that she had an extra ticket to Phantom of the Opera *and wondered if Sally could join her for the matinee. Sally had wanted to see* Phantom *for at least five years, and now she was being offered a free ticket! Dare she call work at the last minute and take a personal leave day, or perhaps call in "sick"? She knew that she wouldn't hesitate a minute to take personal leave if her elderly mother needed her. She also wouldn't hesitate if her pregnant sister needed her to watch "the boys," Sally's nephews, aged two and four. But, to take a day off just for herself...that was another story. Yet, the beautiful music from the play haunted her, and besides, Sally loved the theater. Her second grade class could deal with a substitute for one day, couldn't it?*

Although Sally didn't realize it, she was experiencing a clash in values. Values underlie all conflicts and are the chief determinants of the choices that we make. Sally was a responsible person whose work values included good attendance. She was concerned that her principal would need to find a last-minute substitute for her class. On the other hand, Sally also valued aesthetics. She was intrigued with the glamour and beauty of the musical stage, and the splendorous melodies from Phantom *enchanted her. Family was Sally's highest value, and she would take a day off, even at the last minute, if she was needed by someone near and dear to her. Why, then, did she have so much trouble deciding what to do, even with regards to something that would lift her heart and bring her Self to life?*

The Viennese psychiatrist Viktor Frankl spoke of a hierarchy of values that, from lowest to highest, include values associated with work, values associated with aesthetics or beauty and ultimately values associated with attitudes such as altruism. All three are illustrated in Sally's dilemma, a dilemma that she can successfully resolve only by determining her predominant values. She would have had less of a conflict if one of her work values, that of good attendance, did not have within it an altruistic intent.

> *The grand essentials of happiness are something to do, something to love, and something to hope for.*
>
> —Allan K. Chalmers

 If you had similar choices, what would be your predominant value and how would you have resolved this dilemma?

At a very early age, we begin to experience conflicts in values. The child who wants a wagon and a bicycle for Christmas is told by his parents that he can have only one. When the child really wants both gifts, it is difficult to decide between them, for each choice is tied to his special values. The bicycle will give him independence and a feeling of freedom with the ability to go fast on his own. A wagon is important if he is building a fort or a tree house in the backyard and he needs to haul materials, or if he wants to have fun giving rides to his friends or pets. He chooses by what he values more, or he may find a way of having both. He may use one value to acquire the other—such as hauling things in the wagon for others, receiving pay and then buying a bike on his own.

A woman may experience this same kind of conflict when shopping for a new dress on a limited income. She wants a dress that will be appropriate both for work and for an upcoming party. Once in the store she finds two dresses: an exquisite party dress that won't be appropriate for work, and a fairly nice-looking work dress that will not be special enough for the party. She would like to have both, but can afford only one dress. The work dress is far more practical; the party dress more beautiful. Should she buy the beautiful dress that she will wear infrequently and "make do' with what she has in her closet for work, or upgrade her work wardrobe and "make do" for the party? She wants both. Only one is possible.

> Have you been in this situation and what value
> helped you resolve it?

Both the child's and the woman's conflicts are called *approach-approach conflicts* because both alternatives are desirable. In the situation involving the dress choice, values that relate to beauty, social acceptability and power conflict with values related to practicality and appearance at work. The latter may also be connected to advancement on the job.

Let's suppose that the conflict is between two undesirable choices in what is called *avoidance-avoidance conflict*. Your underlying values are also important here when you want to choose what is the least undesirable. Imagine a young girl, playing dolls at her friend's house. Her friend chooses to play with the newest and best-dressed doll. Two old dolls are left: One is perceived as ugly because some hair is missing, the other as cumbersome because it is big and heavy. In another situation, a young girl is taunted by playmates, but she does not want to fight. She also doesn't want to be called a sissy by the kids just because she is reluctant to fight. Again, values determine the choice of action that she will take.

Lastly, there are *approach-avoidance conflicts* where an undesirable factor is embedded in the desired goal. An example of this is Mary, who wants to marry Bill but doesn't want his mother for a mother-in-law.

Conflicts can occur within ourselves (*intrapsychic*) or *interpersonally* between two or more people, or they can be between a person and an institution. When people take positions expressing their point of view, they are standing up for their underlying values. Let's consider Margaret's story.

> *The future belongs to those who believe in the beauty of their dreams.*
> —Eleanor Roosevelt

MARGARET'S STORY: *When Her Career-Heart Speaks*

Margaret had always wanted to be a social worker. A brilliant woman of forty-nine, she was finally able to begin taking courses at her local community college. Margaret realized that she would be fifty-five years old before she could become a licensed clinical social worker. On the other hand, she could become an aide in two years. In her heart of hearts, this alternative wouldn't be what Margaret wanted most, but she saw it as practical. Though she could afford to attend school for six years, and though she enjoyed school and was a very good student, she doubted the wisdom of beginning a professional career at age fifty-five. Should Margaret listen to the part of her brain that told her she would be too old, or listen to her heart that said, "go on and try it"?

Our value system is always there, but we are not always consciously aware of it. Thus, career counselors spend considerable time with values clarification, to bring to consciousness what is most important to the client. Most people value family, health, high income, security, love, freedom, independence and success. When push comes to shove, what do you value the most? Imagine yourself as a government worker. You took your job for security, and now you are bored. Will you sacrifice security for a job that offers adventure and perhaps high income, but with far less security in the long run? The choice is always as individual as the opportunity you are given.

When you are trying to make decisions related to whether you "should" work or what type of work you want to do, your interests, knowledge and skills play major roles in the process. However, each of these factors must be funneled through your value system—the ultimate determiner of choice. If you were to choose an alternative outside of your values base, you risk self-alienation, which has severe psychological implications. Making choices on the basis of what other people value, whether they are parents, spouses, children or friends, is not a good idea if these choices are in conflict with your own values. When you do act contrary to your own values, you merely trade an interpersonal conflict for an intrapsychic one.

An organizational psychologist, Edgar Schein, talks about career anchors—the values that keep us in place. These values include technical functional competence, general managerial competence, security and stability, creativity, autonomy and independence. Schein also describes lifestyle and pure challenge as career values. The anchors that we are the least willing to pull up are our strongest anchors.

MITCHELL'S STORY: *Anchors Away?*

Mitchell had been a man on the move. He had climbed the career ladder past middle management to high executive status. In so doing, he had physically moved his residence ten times in twice as many years. When he last moved, three years ago, his wife threatened to leave him if it ever happened again. The children were now out of the house and geographic stability was finally a possibility. Margaritte obtained a job in an advertising agency where she has been happy and has received two promotions. With the help of a therapist, Mitch and Margaritte solidified their marriage, purchased a home for the two of them and relaxed into a comfortable lifestyle.

Recently, Mitchell was told by the CEO of his company that he could and should make the move to the top executive position of one of the divisions of the company. However, it entailed making the geographic move from Houston, Texas, to New York State. Such a corporate move appealed to his entrepreneurial creativity and managerial competence. Furthermore, it was pure challenge, another of his values. However, these were not his wife's values. The move might destroy their sense of security together. It would conflict with his own value of their present lifestyle together, and certainly with her own value of it. What anchors would Mitch be willing to pull up? And what anchors would Margaritte be willing to pull up? Lastly, what would this potential change do to their marriage?

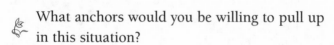 What anchors would you be willing to pull up
in this situation?

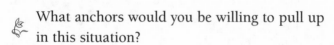 In recent years, these roles have been reversed, thereby making
you the executive on the move. What anchors would your spouse
be willing to pull up?

Soul Values

Our interests, our skills and the knowledge that we have at the time are important bases for decisions that we make. However, our values are even more important because they reside in our soul. As we act on our values, they determine our moral fiber and our spirit. Some people hold

And if you sing as angels and love not the singing, You muffle ears to the voice of the day and the night.

—Kahlil Gibran

values, but they don't act on them when the chips are down. Perhaps they are overly cautious or confused. Other people never seem to get what they want because they are afraid to sacrifice. On the other hand, some people are so self-sacrificing that they are unable to see that life in the world, and even life in their day-to-day world, will continue in their absence. Ultimately, strong values are connected to our sense of meaning in life. The roles we play are based on our inner values, which determine who we are to ourselves, to others within our own traditions, to the institutions of society and to the meaning we give to life itself.

Give Ear to Your Own Voice: Your Unique Interests

Conservatively calculated, the average person spends more than one hundred eighty thousand hours at work throughout his or her lifespan. This does not even include the amount of time spent caring for a home. Approximately one-half of our waking hours are spent working, to say nothing of the time it takes to travel to and from the workplace, or the time it takes to prepare for work, professionally and personally. Because work is such a significant part of life, our heart must be in it. It is critically important for us to enjoy our work and be satisfied with the job that we do. Nothing, absolutely nothing—not money, not security nor the best benefit package in the world—predicts satisfaction in work as reliably as does interest. Where your interests are, so is your heart. John Holland, an expert on people's interests, states that the sum total of our daydreams defines the occupational choice that is consistent with our personality. Where do your daydreams lead you?

*Work!
Thank God for the might of it, The ardor, the urge, the delight of it.*

—Angela Morgan

Valuing Your True Essence along the Journey

According to Holland, all occupations can be classified according to the following six personality types: *realistic, investigative, artistic, social, enterprising* and *conventional.*

Each of these occupational classes or work environments contains tasks that correspond to one of the six personality types:

1. The *realistic* (R) type prefers ordered, explicit and systematic use of objects as would a mechanic or surveyor.
2. The *investigative* (I) type prefers symbolic, observational and creative investigation of cultural and physical phenomenon as would a physicist or chemist.
3. The *artistic* (A) type prefers unsystematized activities with the freedom to manipulate materials, words and people to create products or art forms as would a writer or an artist.
4. The *social* (S) type prefers to enlighten, cure and train others as would a counselor or social science teacher.
5. The *enterprising* (E) type prefers activities requiring the manipulation of others to achieve economic gain or organizational goals as would an executive or a salesperson.
6. The *conventional* (C) type prefers activities requiring ordered, explicit, systematic manipulation of data such as keeping records or operating office machines with economic goals in mind as would a clerk or an accountant.

Furthermore, Holland asserts that people search for occupations that will enable them to use their skills and abilities, to exercise their attitudes and values, and to acquire agreeable problems and roles.

It's fun to look for your own interests. Holland developed an interest inventory, the Self-Directed Search (SDS), that begins by asking about your occupational daydreams. Holland believes that the composite of your personal occupational daydreams will reliably yield your personality type. Richard Nelson Bolles, author of the very popular book *What Color Is Your Parachute?*, created a game called "The Party." This game is widely used to determine a person's Holland Code, such as SAI: Social, Artistic, Investigative.

Players are told to pretend that they are at a party where there are six groups (corresponding to the six code types), each holding a conversation relative to the same topic. However, each group would look at the topic of baseball, for instance, differently. The Artistic group might discuss the ambiance of the newly constructed stadium; the Investigative group would be interested in the statistics such as the RBIs; and the Social group might care more about who comes to the games, getting friends together and such. Each participant is asked which group he or she would like to join first, then second, and finally third. The combination of the three chosen conversations in 1-2-3 order corresponds to a person's Holland Code, which determines the priority of interests such as AIS (Artistic, Investigative, Social), if chosen in the order presented above.

SABRINA'S STORY: *Making Her Dream a Reality*

Sabrina worked in the data processing department of a large international corporation. She didn't hate her work, but often, Sabrina was simply bored. When she saw an advertisement in the paper that her local community college was offering a career development program for women, Sabrina signed up. There she took both the Self-Directed Search and the Strong Interest Inventory. Sabrina realized that her Holland Code was RIC (Realistic, Investigative, Conventional). She also recognized that as a child she enjoyed making things with wood alongside her father who was a carpenter. As a child, Sabrina had wanted to be a carpenter, but her father told her it wasn't woman's work. Back in the late 1960's, Sabrina gave up her dream, but what about now, early in a new century? Sabrina is following her heart. She took early retirement from her company and is now an apprentice carpenter. Fortunately, Sabrina could stop her present work immediately and switch to something more interesting. Beth, on the other hand, completed her change over a considerable period of time.

BETH'S STORY: *Planning the Path to Her Dream*

Beth worked in the comptroller's office of a mid-sized company and she was earning forty-two thousand dollars per year. But, she decided to follow her dream of becoming an elementary school counselor. She knew the change would require a return to school in order to acquire a Master's Degree in school counseling. Beth could not afford to stop working, so she made a five-year plan. Beth decided to begin slowly by taking one course at a time. During this time, she would cut her living expenses by ten thousand dollars a year so that during her fifth year, she could quit her job and do a full-time internship. She informed her employers of her plan and agreed to train her successor. By completing a two-and-a-half-year program in five years, she allowed herself plenty of time to study for her courses. Not only did she graduate with straight A grades, but she was hired by the school in which she interned.

How has all of this change affected Beth's salary? At the time Beth left her previous job she was earning almost fifty thousand dollars a year. She went from fifty thousand to a salary of "zero" income as an intern for one year. She then earned a salary of thirty-one thousand dollars per year as a counselor. Does she miss the bigger income? "Yes and no," Beth says. "I can't

> *Today a new sun rises for me; everything lives, everything is animated, everything seems to speak to me of my passion, everything invites me to cherish it.*
>
> —Anne de Lenclos

> *...living out your dreams only sharpens your sense of what you were looking for.*
> —Jeanne Marie Laskas

buy as much as I used to buy—my cars aren't as new, and my clothing isn't as expensive, but I manage. And, I'm doing what I think that I was born to do, so I feel very, very happy."

Beth's story is a story of planned change, but what if we plan and our plans fall apart. Like Beth, Shirley, a letter carrier, had a dream.

SHIRLEY'S STORY: *Postal Poet*

For as long as Shirley could remember, she wanted to be a writer. In fact, when she graduated from college with a double major in journalism and English, she immediately got a job as a staff writer for a corporate magazine. Shirley felt very lucky. But three years later when she married, Shirley had to leave that job. Her husband, Bill, was transferred to a mid-sized town in the northwest where she was too far away from headquarters to be able to continue in her job.

For awhile, Shirley didn't work outside her home. She was pregnant when the couple moved, and their first child, a boy, was followed two years later by a girl. However, when her husband was forced to take disability leave due to a job-related accident, Shirley felt obliged to return to work. She took the postal exam, passed it, and was hired almost immediately as a mail handler.

Though Shirley was glad enough to work, she needed more to stimulate her mind. After two years, Shirley thought she would go crazy if there was nothing more in her life than mountains of mail at work and laundry at home. Shirley began to write poetry, and she began to use her mind dexterously. She formed meter and rhyme, molding words in her head while performing menial tasks with her hands. Eventually, she com-

piled a book of her poetry that she one day hopes to publish. She began sending her verses to journals, trusting that one day an editor would value her efforts. She even entered a poetry contest.

Shirley came to the important realization that if she cannot express her interests through paid work, she must express them elsewhere in order to be a whole person. Career was more than a job to her—it was all the roles that she played, whether for work or leisure.

Interests, because they are part of who we are as persons, generally last through a lifetime. As children we express our interests in our play. Consider the forensic psychiatrist who used to play spy and intrigue games. As a child she always tried to figure out "Who done it?" and "Why?" Or, the woman, who took up oil painting in her late forties subsequent to divorce after a twenty-five year marriage. She remembered that as a child she loved art, but she had given it up in her twenties when her husband suggested that she had little talent. Genuine interests show themselves early, and remain late.

> *Look at everything*
> *as though you were*
> *seeing it either*
> *for the first or the last time.*
> *Then your time on*
> *earth will be filled*
> *with glory.*
>
> —Betty Smith

Interests cry out to be released. The people who love what they do, love it because what they do is what they want to do, what inwardly they feel called to do. Vocation is not only for those in religious life; vocation is for each of us.

We are called by our interests to use our abilities—our talents, whether those talents are writing, parenting, counseling, counting or cooking. Joseph Campbell said," Follow your bliss!" In the scripture it is written, "let your light shine," (Matt 5:16, Modern Language Bible)

> *Open the envelope of your soul*
> *to discern God's orders hidden there.*
>
> —Marian Wright Edelman

and to paraphrase Jiminy Cricket, "Always let your interests be your guide."

Our connections to others are often based on our mutual interests, but caring for one another may be the more important underlying value. We can enjoy each other even when we have different interests.

LEE'S STORY: *Death and Baseball—It All Happens Together*

My best friend died four years ago. In her life, Margie had been an avid baseball fan. She taught me, if not to like, then at least to tolerate the sport. We had a joke between us. I enjoyed opera; she enjoyed baseball. I took her to the opera, and she learned to say "Bravo" when something magnificent was sung. I never quite learned to shout "Charge" at the ballpark. Margie called to my attention that the movement of baseball players was like a dance: that they stretched tremendous distances to catch a ball and that their movements were as graceful yet powerful as those of ballet masters.

The year before she died, Margie planned a very special event. She was going to take fifteen of her closest friends to watch the Baltimore Orioles play a very important ball game at Camden Yards. I do not remember what team they were playing, but I know that the Orioles won the pennant that year. Sadly, my friend, who mightily and diligently fought hepatitis for the previous three years, died the morning of the game.

Few of her fifteen friends went to the game that night, but I knew that I had to go. Going was the only way that I could feel Margie's presence on the day that she had left this earth.

I realize now that my family accompanied me to that game—my son, a daughter, a son-in-law—because they weren't sure that I could make it on my own. But I sat there through four innings and felt Margie sitting beside me, and then I left without her. Death and baseball, somehow or other it all happens together. Though death has taken her from me, when I now think of baseball, I remember her joy at the games, a joy that brings me to life.

How to, When and Why: Knowledge and Skill

Not too many years ago, a journalist was asked to write a "how-to" article that was related to both aging and the Christmas season. The article dealt with ways to celebrate the holidays after the loss of a loved one. In order to write the article, the journalist had to look at her own personal experiences of both celebration and loss, and then to explore the experiences of others, as well as to assess the opinions of experts.

When we make any basic life decision, we need to do much the same as the journalist did in preparing to write her article. To begin, we must search our knowledge, i.e., "What do I know?", and assess our skill, that is, "What can I do?" Often, knowledge and skill are interrelated, but not always.

Knowledge comes from having a direct understanding of something. This awareness can be gained through experience, through association, or through reasoning, as in the comprehension of a fact. However, the word "knowledge" always implies being aware, and it infers awareness of internal as well as external events.

Skill is the ability to use our knowledge effectively. It is the competent doing of learned tasks. Interestingly, the Book of Deuteronomy tells us that when the Ten Commandments were given to the Israelites they were told to know them and to do them. This implies that there is a moral imperative to act when what we know will benefit self or others.

When you are thinking about finding work, you should ask yourself, "What do I know, and what can I do?" "What do I know about myself, and what do I know about the world of work?" "What skills do I possess that would be useful in the world of work, and which of these skills do I wish to utilize?" "Which skills do I enjoy using, and which would I enjoy using if I had more ability?" And lastly, "What knowledge and skills that I do not have now, would I want to acquire in order to do a specific kind of work?"

CAROL AND ALICE'S STORY: *Whose Wishes? Whose Dreams?*

Consider this story about two physicians. Carol "aced" her way through college, went to her father's alma mater to obtain her medical degree, interned at a prestigious hospital, and completed her residency in obstetrics and gynecology. After graduation, Carol joined her father's practice, only to realize, upon his retirement some ten years later, that she had done it all to please him. When her father died, Carol sold the practice. Though study and work had come very easily for her, Carol retired from the practice of medicine and opened a flower shop and nursery which she enjoys to this day.

> *Once you have a dream...you're on your way. A goal is just a dream with a deadline.*
>
> *—Lorraine Hale*

The second physician always wanted to practice medicine—surgery to be exact. As a child, Alice conducted "pretend" operations with anyone who would play "doctor" with her. When she graduated from high school, Alice was unable to obtain a scholarship to her state university, and because of her family's finances, she went to a local community college instead. Upon graduation, Alice attended a state college where she majored in Biology. Although she graduated with a B+ average, Alice was not admitted to medical school. However, she didn't forsake her dream. She applied and was accepted into a graduate Biology program at a second-rate school. But Alice studied hard, and completed an interesting thesis. Alice applied to medical school again, and although she didn't get into her top three choices, she was accepted into a lesser-known school. Again, she studied hard, graduated, and completed her internship. Alice then applied for a post-doctoral fellowship in a very specific area that involved medicine and biomedical engineering. She thought that by completing this one-year fellowship she would have a better chance of getting a first-rate residency in surgery, which proved to be true. Today Alice is on the surgical faculty of one of the nation's top medical schools. Her path took her almost seventeen years of formal schooling beyond high school, but to her it was worthwhile.

Strange as it may seem, these two doctors have much in common. Though Carol breezed through school and Alice struggled, though Alice remained a physician and Carol did not, both of these women acted on what they knew about themselves as that knowledge unfolded.

When any of us acts, we act not simply as individuals but as a complex combination of ourselves, of the others in our lives, and of our circumstances.

Try as we may, we can never get away from the fact that the opportunities the world has to offer are always mediated by the circumstances in which we find ourselves. Through effort we can alter our circumstances, but in so doing there are always others involved. These others may be alive and around us, like our spouses and children. They may be a part of our past, like parents and grandparents, former spouses and lovers, who have left us with memories and wisdom, or perhaps have left us with the remnants of their dysfunctional behavior. Nevertheless, they remain with us as part of who we are and of what we know and, thus, come to play a part in our choices, and in what we do with our lives.

EUNICE'S STORY: *Desire and Choice*

Eunice, a young geologist living on the east coast, won a doctoral scholarship to a renowned university in the Midwest. Had she not been married with children, she would have taken the scholarship in the blink of an eye. In fact, until the last minute, Eunice thought she would accept it. She told herself that she would take her kids with her, and she would meet with her husband, William James, whenever she could. Some of her friends urged her to do this, but Eunice knew in her heart of hearts that she didn't want to leave "W. J." and that he didn't want her to go either. So, she passed up an opportunity that she knew would not come again.

This would have been a poor decision if Eunice were to blame W. J. or herself. Her "sacrifice" would have taken its toll on her family life in years to come. Knowledge of ourselves and of our desires includes a knowledge of our circumstances and of those whom we love.

MARY'S STORY: *Need to Change*

Mary is a woman with a high need for achievement and change. She also has a need to defer to others. Her husband, to whom she usually defers, dislikes change and does not want Mary to achieve independently. In fact, he wants her to conform to his way in everything from how to roll the toothpaste tube, to where and when to go out—as well as with whom. Mary and Ted married when they were young. Though "in love," psychologically they were not well matched. Now that the children are in school, Mary wants to finish her college education, but she fears that it will compromise her marriage.

> *Magic is believing in yourself.*
> *If you can do that, you can make anything happen.*
>
> —Foka Gomez

Furthermore, Mary is not confident in her skills. Like many women she suffers from "math anxiety." Mary had always heard that women were not good in math and so she avoided advanced algebra and trigonometry in high school, even though her college admission test showed that she had a fairly high math aptitude. Like Mary, most of us can acquire the ability to do just about anything if we have the interest, the willingness to apply ourselves to the learning tasks, and self-confidence. However, Mary's lack of confidence in herself, plus her tendency to defer to a husband who doesn't want her to achieve independently is at cross-purposes with her inner need to achieve. Mary may need professional counseling to help her gain the knowledge and skill to build her confidence and achieve independently. She and her husband jointly may need marriage counseling as Mary may confront Ted as her confidence increases. She may even decide to squeeze the toothpaste tube and not roll it at all.

Just as we have varied interests, when we think of the world of work, we should consider the various types of abilities or skills involved. There are mechanical and physical abilities, spatial abilities, investigative or scientific abilities, artistic and social abilities, and enterprising abilities that relate to managerial and sales skills. There are also clerical skills, which are often called conventional abilities. Note that these abilities correspond to interests and the Holland Code. When job hunting, you might ask yourself which skills you have in sufficient amount, and which skills you might like to augment and how they relate to your interests.

Ray Ziegler, a late renowned career counselor and a friend of Lee's, used to say that if you really want to inventory your skills you should list everything that you have done, from mowing the lawn to driving the car pool, and everything on which you have ever been complimented by others. Then you should categorize the list, which for most people would be surprisingly long. The career development journey can thus be viewed as a process of learning about self, the world of work, and decision making. Knowledge and skill, coupled with interest, and filtered through values, gives you a head start on the trip.

Your virtual question involves your highest heart quest. Where is the greatest meaning in your life? What is the overarching value that guides your lifelong journey? You may still be searching for the answers to these questions, and you will not be alone. As you continue through the chapters in this book, we hope you will gather a special insight into your heart's delight.

In the next chapter on the wonder of space and time, you will begin to appreciate the value of fallow time.

HIGHLIGHTS

Follow your heart to find your true values...

Believe in the beauty of your dreams...

Give ear to your own voice...

Appreciate those people who encourage you...

Be true to your soul values...

Express your interests and skills...

Allow your trueSelf, your lifeSpirit to evolve in your work...

Find your highest heart quest...

Put in all of your heart and soul...

PERSONAL REFLECTIONS

1. In this chapter, we talk about values. Below is a list of ten basic values shared by many people. There is a space for you to add a value that may be very important to you that is not on this list. Rank the list according to the importance of your own values, with number 1 as your most important value and number 10 (or number 11 if you add another) as your least important value. (This is a forced-choice exercise that some people find difficult to do. We encourage you to try this because it may help you better understand your own values and value conflicts.)

VALUE	RANK ORDER
Family	
Health	
Money	
Security	
Love	
Freedom	
Pleasure	
Spiritual	
Independence	
Success	

Valuing Your True Essence along the Journey

After you complete your ranking, you may wish to answer the following questions.

- Are you surprised by how you ranked your values?

- What have you learned about yourself that you did not know before?

- How does this values exercise help you to understand some of the values conflicts you have had or are having in your life?

- How does this values exercise help you understand some of the decisions you have made in your life?

2. Several types of conflicts were discussed in this chapter. *Approach–approach* conflicts occur when both alternatives are desirable. *Avoidance–avoidance* conflicts occur when neither alternative is desirable and one must be chosen. *Approach–avoidance* conflicts occur when there is an undesirable factor embedded in the desired goal. Think of some examples of these types of values conflicts in your own life.

Approach–Approach	
Avoidance–Avoidance	
Approach–Avoidance	

Which type of conflict is hardest for you to resolve? Why?

3. Take either Dr. John Holland's Self-Directed Search (SDS), or do the exercise "The Party" in Richard Bolles's book *What Color Is Your Parachute?* to determine your interest personality preferences. After deciding on your interest preferences, examine how they are reflected in the work that you do. Where are the "fits" or "misfits" in your work life?

4. If you are thinking about finding work or changing to different work, spend some time thinking about and answering these basic questions:

   • What do I know (knowledge)—about myself, about the world of work?

   • What can I do (skills)? What skills do I possess that would be useful in the world of work? What skills do I enjoy using, and which would I enjoy using if I had more ability? Are there knowledge and skills that I do not have now but would want to acquire in order to do a specific kind of work?

5. Edgar Schein defines "career anchors" as the values that keep us in place. The anchors that we are least willing to pull up are our strongest career anchors. Which career anchors are you unwilling to pull up? What examples are there from your life concerning the impact of your own career anchors?

6. Although we can try to alter our circumstances, there are always others involved in our lives who have an impact on and are impacted by our decisions. Who are these significant others in your life and what part have they played in your past choices? What part do they play in your choices now?

What Brings You to Life?

"A wonderful light feeling when I realize that I don't have to do
  something: I have a choice"

"Feeling free as a kite unleashed"

"Quiet time with freedom to explore an idea"

"Experiencing wondrous nature—basking in the beauty of our natural earth, relaxing in its peacefulness"

"Mountains; a beautiful sunset—sitting by a lake"

"Quiet time to read a good book, just for fun"

"Getting it all done within the allotted time"

"A clean house"; "Someone coming to clean for me"

"Financial stability"

"Vacation and travel to see new sights and people"

"Special shopping, such as buying china in England"

"Going out on my porch on nice days when home due to
  my illness"

"Drives to rural areas"

"Finding special shells on the beach, even beach glass:
  fragments worn smooth"

"Clear blue sky; bright stars"

"Inner joy!"

"The quality of light and shadows through trees
  and in people"

What Brings You to Life?

"Being present in the moment: not worried about the past or
   future"

"Being alone"; "sitting"

"This class I'm taking on self-care–Thanks !"

"Sleep"; "Rest"

"Bare arms above the hot tub"

"Silence"; "Writing an excellent poem"

"A whole self-care day–such a release; time in my sewing room,
   husband doing car pool, etc."

"Unexpected free days away with husband"

"Unexpected company that we like"

"Three-day weekends off from work"

"Being in the mountains; filling my lungs with clean fresh air"

4

The Wonder of Space and Time: A Gift to Womanhood

Beauty and Grace are performed whether or not we will
or sense them. The least we can do is try to be there.
—Annie Dillard

Of Time and Space and Womanhood

One of the things that really puzzles people is time. Though we don't like the thought, each of us knows that we are given just so much of it. And what time we have we experience as fickle. It seems to go by so quickly when we are enjoying ourselves. When we are having fun we want to stop the clock, or at least slow things down. On the other hand, we want to speed things up when we are uncomfortable or bored. When we are children we perceive time as an endless wasteland. We can't wait until we are grown up so that each of us can take control of our "destiny." But when in our older years, it seems like only minutes ago that we were children playing on the seesaw or making castles in the sand. The years, the decades, went by so fast!

> *At...times, our spiritual windows may need to be opened to let in fresh breezes in the form of laughter, meditation, prayer and play.*
>
> —Beverly Elaine Eanes

We have been told by the wise people that there is such a thing as the "right" time. We read in Ecclesiastes (3:1-8), that "there is a season, and a time for every matter under heaven: a time to be born, and a time to die; a time to plant, and a time to pluck up what is planted; a time to kill, and a time to heal... a time to mourn, and a time to dance...a time for war, and a time for peace." And, though we are told that there is a right time, so often we don't know what the right time is. What, for instance, is the right time to marry, to have children, to study, to vacation, to retire? Often, when we arrive at the time, the opportunity isn't there, or it's there and we don't want to take it.

As women we sometimes tell time in lunar months by our menstrual cycles and by our childbearing years. We also tell time by graying hair, and by when we first feel the desire to color it. We tell time by breasts that begin to sag so that a bra is an absolute necessity, as well as by the day that we forced our mothers to buy us our first "training bra" when there was no necessity for it at all.

But as much as this is true, it is also true that we can psychologically step out of time. What happened to us twenty, thirty years ago can be as recent in our minds as what happened ten minutes ago, especially when feelings are involved. We can see again at age thirty-five the boy, now man, that gave us our first kiss at thirteen. And if we then had a crush on him, we blush all over again. Feelings cannot and do not tell time. They simply are. And like eternity, they are always now.

Time and Memory

Canon Jacques Leclerq wrote something profound about time and memory. A translation of Leclerq's words by Fergus Murphy goes something like this. When we don't live life instinctively we are governed by thought. Thought takes place in time. To make a scientific discovery, run a business or cook a meal takes thought. And what is conducive to thought is solitude. When we are alone we think.

Wise philosophers have taught us that when we think, when we reflect and remember past things, we sometimes feel joy or pain. If we would relive joy, we must first remember it, and to do this we journey inward and backward. To remove pain, we must also journey inward and backward, for it is only by reliving it in memory that we can permanently rid ourselves of it. Although we frequently try to drown pain in the deep well of forgetfulness, it rises to the surface again and again until we face it and resolve its hold on us. Just as pain is the way in to sorrow, so is pain the way out. There is no escape. But there is the healing of memories, when we are ready for healing to take place.

A group of women were talking about their divorces and how these now affected their college-aged children, even though each of their divorces occurred before their children were four years old. One woman, whose divorce occurred when her daughter was two years old, said that her child had been adopted at the age of two months. Though now a young adult, the child still suffered serious abandonment issues. The mother, a professional counselor, said that every time she tried to get her daughter to a therapist, the young woman replied that she was not yet ready to recycle back, enter her pain and receive the "healing of memories." For the daughter, the right time has not yet occurred for her to reenter pain.

The mother had entered her own pain, and had come out on the other side. Therefore, she could let go and wait. The mother said the following: "My marriage was right for me at twenty, but wrong for me at twenty-eight. I had grown and had gone to a different place at twenty-eight than the place that I was in at twenty. My husband still wanted me to be twenty. I couldn't do it; the marriage couldn't work."

A woman's needs and wants can be very different at different phases of her life. To exemplify such a change, listen to what a recent widow said of her marriage and herself. "Jim and I were soul mates. I couldn't imagine life without him. I never even thought of myself as single and without my mate. Then he got sick and was dead in three weeks. A rare virus took him. Now I can't think of myself with a mate. I still go places, but I go alone. I know that Jim is dead, but in a way he is still close. At this time, I don't even want to think of being with someone else. When he was alive, I never wanted to be alone. Now I cherish my aloneness."

> *Solitude is the richness of self,*
> *and loneliness is the poverty of self.*
> —May Sarton

SAUL'S STORY: *What Really Matters over Time*

When time is precious, we need to recognize the importance of being with loved ones. Consider the story of Saul, who was a senior rabbi and a meticulous record keeper who had been the sole clergyman of a large congregation for close to thirty years. Once, after the congregation had hired an assistant rabbi, Saul took his young assistant into his office. There the older man showed his young assistant the extensive files of all of those people in the congregation who had been born or married, as well as those who had died during his tenure. The younger rabbi was impressed and suggested that the senior rabbi must have seen and heard everything. Saul shook his head from side to side. "No," he said, "not everything. Although the most frequent wish of a dying man or woman is for more time, I have never heard a dying man say, "I need more time to cut the grass,' or "to wash the car,' nor a dying woman say "I need more time to get my hair done.'" Then the older rabbi gently told the younger man that

78

what he did hear people say is that they wished they had more time to spend with loved ones or to see or hear beautiful things.

Any of us can go to an art gallery to see the exhibit of a master artist and invariably we will see some women race from room to room, hardly seeing the beauty that is there, lest they miss a single painting, realizing not at all that they have missed the whole thing. Contrast these women with those who linger over a single piece of work, letting the beauty of every detail soak in, savoring the moment and thinking of nothing else. Perhaps these women did not get to see every room, but they certainly saw the exhibit!

> *Most of what we do doesn't need to be done anyway— at least not today.*
> —Glen Dromgoole

Consider also the mother who is so concerned that her children behave in one way or another that she misses the delightful mischievous smile on the face of her two-year-old son when he thinks he has finally put one over on his older brother. Contemplation takes time, but it also takes us out of time. It is in the contemplation of the ever-so-small that our mind is lifted to the mind of God.

> *Soak it into your soul!*
> —Beverly Elaine Eanes

Our Own Special Space

Perhaps you remember the legend of the "idiot" woman. Supposedly she was a medieval virgin who lived in a monastery. The other nuns made fun of her because she seemed to enjoy working in the kitchen. She wore a rag around her head, ate only the crumbs she picked up, drank water from the pots and pans she scoured. She was thought odd by those with whom she lived and was made fun of by them. One day an angel visited a highly regarded holy man who lived in a mountain monastery in a nearby village. The angel told the monk to come down from his high place and visit the monastery where the "idiot" woman lived because she was truly blessed. The monk did as the angel commanded, but when he reached the convent, the nuns did not want him to see the odd woman. Instead, they told him about all of her quirks. Finally, the monk revealed that an angel had told him about the blessedness of the woman of whom the nuns had made fun. Truly repentant, the nuns began to beg forgiveness of the woman and to venerate her. Thereupon she left the monastery never to be seen by the nuns again.

This simple story says something about both time and space. Both in ridiculing and venerating the "idiot" woman, the women who lived with her spent their time seeing only surface things. The women were so busy looking at her idiosyncrasies that they never took the time to see for themselves what the woman saw herself. On the other hand, the "idiot" woman could not be revered and stay her simple self, so she went to a different, perhaps even smaller space in order to continue her vision.

> *Space, like time, engenders forgetfulness; but it does so by setting us bodily free from our surroundings and giving us back our primitive unattached state.*
>
> —Thomas Mann

Dreamers can stay in one space and wander the earth. Scientists from the sanctum of their laboratories have uncovered a vast universe of unparalleled complexity and beauty. Hermit saints from the smallest cells have stormed the heavens. John Chalberg, a Minnesotan who travels the United States and Canada, does a monologue about this kind of thinking called, "An Evening with G. K. Chesterton." As Chesterton, he says, "Only in small spaces, can you really comprehend big ideas." Therefore, "small worlds are the only worlds worth inhabiting."

What does this mean to modern women? It means we don't always have to be "out there," nor do we always have to rush. We need the freedom to be and the space to receive life. Sometimes like seeds, we need fallow time. Like seeds, we need the time of autumn and winter in order to bud in spring and flower in summer. It also means that we don't have to feel guilty when we stand and wait, or when we rest. It means that what we see from our seat in front of the computer or from our kitchen window may be as significant or perhaps even more so than what some others see from their

> *Just to be is a blessing.*
> *Just to live is holy.*
> —Abraham Joshua Heschel

mountaintops or skyscrapers. It means that what we do when we brush a child's hair, fix her shoestring or mend his tie may be as powerful an activity as that of any power broker on Wall Street. It also means that if Mary Modern is the power broker on Wall Street, as she well may be, her actions on the job may be no more or less significant than the hello that she gives her partner when she gets home. It means that if we as women take the time to retreat, which means to return to ourselves and recollect, we intrinsically will know what the poet Edna St. Vincent (Millay) knew at age seventeen, when she wrote:

> The world stands out on either side
> No wider than the heart is wide...
> Above the earth there stands the sky
> No wider than the soul is high...
> God, I can push the grass apart
> And lay my fingers on your heart.

It is no accident that in the Old Testament the Holy Spirit of God, the *Shekinah,* is feminine. It is no accident that *El Shadda* (name for God) means in Hebrew "the breasted one." Nor is it an accident that *Sophia* (the Greek word Wisdom) in the Septuagint Bible is also feminine. Women have always been of the earth, spiritual and wise. What we as women throughout time have always had in common is that our work as women has forged the future of humanity. In creating and maintaining life we are akin to the very breath of God that creates and maintains all of life.

The soul has been compared by spiritual writers to a sack in which grain is poured. The sack is simply a receptacle, but the amount of grain that can be poured into it varies with the openness of the sack.

How open is the twenty-first-century woman to taking the time to think about time, and to recognize that the right time to love and cherish always is now? How open is the twenty-first-century woman to taking the time to ponder space as more than just a physical entity, but also to seeing it in its political, psychological and social aspects and to recognizing that "small" can be "very large" indeed? Each woman needs to set aside the time to discern what she wants in life

> *To keep the lamp burning,*
> *we have to keep putting oil in it.*
> —Mother Teresa

and to separate or reconcile that desire with what she wanted before and with what others have wanted for her. Take a moment to consider this: We can be in touch with the whole world in seconds; what time do we take to be in touch with ourselves?

GEORGINE'S STORY: *Flying Free Again*

Such is the case with Georgine, who used to be a pilot, as was her husband, Charles. Both professional consultants, they flew their own plane to "jobs" in various cities. One day, while Georgine was flying the plane, one of the engines blew. The oil spilled over the window as flames darted about the plane. Fortunately, this story has a happy ending. She was able to safely land her aircraft as her copilot husband looked out of the window on his side and guided her down. After that experience Georgine refused to fly again. Other pilots tried to convince her that she should go back up. "If you don't do it now, you never will," they told her. But Georgine didn't listen. She didn't care. She, like the "idiot" woman in the convent, simply walked away. Other people saw Georgine

> *So much has been given to me; I have no time to ponder over that which has been denied.*
> —Helen Keller

the pilot. They never saw what she was looking at: her freedom. They didn't know that she could see it whether she was flying the plane or she wasn't. At one time flying gave her freedom, but to make her fly now would be to take away her freedom.

Time and space for ourselves gives each of us freedom. There is a place for us and we as women need only go inside ourselves to connect with the wider world. There is also a time for us, as there is a time for every purpose under heaven. Because we are a part of that purpose, the time for us is now. Let us not feel guilty for taking it.

If you surrender completely to the moments as they pass, you live more richly those moments.

—Anne Morrow Lindbergh

HIGHLIGHTS

Take time for your soul to blossom...

Let the fresh breeze flow through your "spiritual windows"...

Allow the memories time to heal...

Cherish solitude...

Share time and space with your loved ones...

Revel in your wacky quirks...

Appreciate your simple moments...

Make time for the earth within to nourish the seed...

Walk gently around in your inner space...

It is time for you, now!...

Find a special spot...sit...ponder...

PERSONAL REFLECTIONS

1. Think of your own sense of "time." Considering your personal circumstances, describe your sense of "time" in words, or phrases.

2. The following quote from *Sabbath Time* by Tilden Edwards speaks to our culture's unhealthy drivenness/escapism rhythm of time.

> *Nearly everyone senses that work alone is not sufficient for human fulfillment. One of the sad ironies of this situation is that, despite our intentions to allow a different quality of time in our lives, we often end up turning all our time into work time....The rhythm of life for countless people, set up by this culturally pressured way, thus emerges as one that oscillates between driven achievement (both on and off the job) and some form of mind-numbing private escape.*

Now, think about how you spend your time in an average day/week and reflect on the following questions:

- Are you satisfied with the quality of how you use your time?

- Are there some aspects of your life/values that are being neglected? If so, name a few.

- Is there time for you to do (or Be) what you need for yourself? for others?

- Can you allow yourself fallow time?

- If you realize you aren't living your time the way you want, what changes can you make to fit your needs better?

3. Thich Nhat Hanh has written many books about the Buddhist teachings of mindfulness—of being truly present in the moment. He warns us, "If we are not fully ourselves, truly in the present moment, we miss everything." In his books he gives suggestions about ways to practice mindfulness. "We try to be in touch with life and look deeply as we drink our tea, walk, sit down or arrange flowers. The secret of the success is that you are really yourself, and when you are really yourself, you can encounter life in the present moment."

- Are you able to truly Be Present to the moment?

- What helps you do this?

- What hinders you from doing this?

4. The following quote is attributed to Mohandas Gandhi: "I am my message." What message is your life saying to you and to those around you?

What Brings You to Life?

"Looking at farm scenes: fields, windmills, barns and silos"

"Beautiful blue water"

"Pictures of sailboats"

"Seeing God work in people's lives when they help one another"

"Presiding at the Eucharist"

"Scripture from the Bible"

"Spiritual gifts: music, poetry, tender moments or stories"

"Recognizing God at work in my life"

"Freedom in worship"

"Praise music"

"Prayer, meditation"

"Helping others, serving God"

"Religious services: spoken word of God; singing praises"

"Christmas"

"Gospel music"

"Church services"

"I am on a joy journey"

"Rainbows of promise–beautiful gifts of God"

"Sunday school class"

What Brings You to Life?

"Reading or meditating in the Bishop's Garden at the Cathedral"

"Retreats"

"Reading encouraging scriptures"

"Bringing joy to a person in pain through caring, listening and prayer"

"Communicating with a congregation through preaching my passionate beliefs"

"Seeing how the Lord is working in my life: spirit-filled"

"The transcendent nature of the human spirit enlivens my spirit"

5

God, the Sacred
and WomanSoul

The voice of the deep feminine is beginning to speak
   clearly and firmly
to many women. And it is by sharing our inner
   truths, our sacred truths,
with each other that...an untraditional perspective
   about what it means
to live an embodied spirituality in the world today,
   is beginning to take form.
                    —Patricia Hopkins

Birthing WomanSoul

We embrace the sacred art of birthing WomanSoul, bringing the soul of women to life. The sacred essence of women is born in the everyday spirituality that encompasses all of precious life. A recent study of very high-achieving women stated that eight out of nine women considered themselves to be spiritual, but only two of these nine remained religious. When queried, the others said that they could not relate to the patriarchal form of religion that was practiced in their church of origin. Calling God "Lord" and praying to "Him" in a church where most of "His" ministers and priests were men has become very difficult, if not impossible, for them, even though the great majority of these women believe in God, Creator and Redeemer, and believe that the Spirit of God is omnipresent.

Recently, a Reform Jewish woman attended an Orthodox Jewish service on the holiday of Simchat Torah. On this holiday Jews "rejoice in the Law," and traditionally on this occasion they complete the reading of the Book of Deuteronomy and begin reading the Book of Genesis anew so that each year the Torah is read in its entirety. Also, on this special occasion all of the scrolls in the synagogue are removed from the Ark, where they are kept, and are carried around the synagogue seven times. Traditionally, it is men who carry them, but in Reform temples, women now also carry the scrolls.

The Reform Jewish woman at this particular Jewish service later stated that for the first time the Orthodox congregation allowed the women to carry Torahs in a special Hakafot (walk around the synagogue). They had added this eighth walk just for the women. She related that the women virtually danced up the aisles of the synagogue. They carried the heavy scrolls as if they were lovingly holding babies in their arms as they twirled to the sound of their own singing. She said that their joy was beautiful to behold. "It was," she said, "as though shackles around their heels had been released." And then she added, "I wonder how many more years will have to pass before the women are no longer added on, but one of the seven."

It is true today that within Reform and Conservative Judaism women are now counted "one of the seven." Women and men also sit together in worship, which they do not do in Orthodox Judaism, where it is believed that it is best for men and women to pray separately as each person must relate to God in his or her own way without distraction. There are also female Reform and Conservative cantors and rabbis. But the professional clergywomen are not unlike many of their Protestant Christian sisters in that they are often relegated to smaller congregations or serve as assistants to male clergy. Whether there is separation or relegation, the female spirit is vital.

Nevertheless, women remain as spiritual as ever, for they know that there is more to life than can be fully seen or understood. Women recognize the transcendent and live the authentic. Many religious women today frequently address God in a way that is nonlimiting. *Creator, Redeemer, Spirit, Presence, Higher Power, Great Creature of Centeredness, Divine Mystery, God of a Thousand Names* are some of the words that are used. Just as *Master, Lord* and *Father* are words that have been used for generations (and many women still use these terms), new names such as *Mother, Sister* and *Friend* are used by many modern women and men when speaking to or about the Deity.

> *Without faith, nothing is possible. With it, nothing is impossible.*
> —Mary McLeod Bethune

LEE'S STORY: *Yah*

A friend, a Roman Catholic nun, was musing in her journal about how to address God. She wrote, "What can I call you when I talk to you in prayer? Should I call you Yahweh, the One Who Is and Who Will Be? That is such a formal name, and one so full of Awe that even the Hebrew High Priest says it only once a year in the Holy of Holies. No, Yahweh is too distant for me. I see you as friend, and yet I adore you. I know! I will call you Yah. Yah, my adorable friend."

What Brings You to Life?

LEE'S STORY: *Chair Prayer*

The above excerpt illustrates a deep connection between a woman and her Creator, Redeemer, and Friend. It is a connection that remains unbroken from birth to eternity though the connection is not always apparent to us. The sister who mused in her journal about "Yah" was actually in prayer, but so was another nun who came to see a psychotherapist because she couldn't pray. The therapist told her to pretend that the empty chair in the office was God, and to tell the empty chair all of the "I can'ts" that she had told the therapist. The woman faced the chair and said, "I can't pray, and I can't stand it that I can't pray!" A whole litany of can'ts began to flow from the woman's mouth, as tears welled in her eyes. Then the woman realized that her dialogue with the chair was actually a prayer to God, the One Who Hears, and her tears were an awareness that the invisible connection was still unbroken.

> *Prayer is exhaling the spirit of man and inhaling the spirit of God.*
> —Edwin Keith

JEAN'S STORY: *Halos Aren't Really Necessary*

As a child, I remember thinking that prayer was sitting on a hard pew in church with my eyes closed, my hands folded piously together, with an angelic look on my face, and maybe even the sunlight streaming in through the stained-glass windows glowing around my head like a halo. That was how I pictured prayer. Unfortunately, I was often bored and restless in church, and my behavior couldn't hope to match this picture. I was certain that I didn't know how to pray.

Now, I can chuckle about this childhood picture of prayer, but actually it's a pretty good example of what happens to any of us when we have such a narrow definition or picture of something. It can result in feeling excluded or feeling discouraged about ourselves or feeling incapable of ever being able to do something "right" or "good enough." Many girls and women worry about inadequacies in any case, but prayer is an area in which many people feel dispirited.

What do I think about prayer now? I see prayer as the way we develop our personal relationship with God, our way of inviting God into our hearts. Prayer can be our way to praise God, to express our thankfulness to God or to intercede with God for ourselves and others. Basically, prayer is our intentional opening to God's presence with our whole selves. We are asked to bring ourselves before God in prayer as we are—not as we want to be, nor as we think we should be. It's a "come as you are party" to connect truly with God. Thank heavens, no more folded hands and pious expression for me.

> Spiritual power can be seen in a person's reverence for life—hers and all others, including animals and nature.
>
> —Virginia Satir

I experience prayer in so many different ways now. For me, prayer comes through openness to the present moment. Prayer can happen in church on Sunday morning, but prayer can also happen sitting on my deck watching a chickadee fly back and forth to the bird feeder. Or, prayer can be taking my dog for a walk and letting myself experience her joyful sniffing, her moment-by-moment encounter with all the creatures she meets on the path. Or, prayer can be writing a Dear God letter in my journal. Sometimes, prayer can be sitting across from someone I don't like very much and becoming aware of the judgmental thoughts racing through my brain. Then, miraculously taking a deep breath and silently saying to myself and to God, "We humans come in all shapes, sizes, personalities and whims. Help me accept people who reflect the many ways you've made us."

Prayer isn't my childhood picture of "doing it right" anymore. Instead, prayer is a willingness to let myself be changed.

BEV'S STORY: *True Spirit*

When I was a child I heard about something called the Trinity, that God was three persons in one. I didn't know how that was possible, but since God was special, He probably could do anything. After all, He made the whole amazing world and everything in it, didn't He? However, I became somewhat alarmed at the further explanations of the three persons: God the Father, God the Son and God the Holy Ghost. It was this last word that struck terror in my child's heart. Holy or not, He was still a ghost! No amount of explanation seemed to help. I loved God the Father, who was so special, and Jesus his son, who loved little children, but that was enough.

> Bidden or not Bidden,
> God is present.
> —Carl Jung

When I explained this to Jean and Lee, they almost simultaneously said, "So, you thought of God as two guys and a scary ghost." I looked at them and was startled to realize that indeed it had been true. However, in my later childhood years I learned that the term Holy Ghost *also meant "Holy Spirit," and this latter term really lightened my heart. It was this Spirit for whom I found a true affinity as I began to think of the Holy Spirit in feminine images. After all, Mary, who was Jesus' mother, and many of the women in the Bible were very spiritual. And, this feminine aspect of God gave a wonderful balance to the Trinity. Words describing the Holy Spirit:* Counselor, Teacher, *and* Spirit of truth *(John 14:26, 15:26) also sounded like many of the wonderful wise women that I knew.*

Perhaps it is not surprising that Bev became first a nurse, then a nurse-midwife, and then a pastoral counselor who also taught in each of those fields. The attributes of her own spirit evolved into helping others to improve their well-being. How children learn of God can have a significant impact on their lives. It behooves parents and spiritual leaders to listen

It is the Spirit that most clearly introduces a feminine element into the Christian understanding of God....
The Spirit brooding on the waters, travailing in the creation, building unity and wholeness, most clearly suggests the feminine principle...

—John Macquarrie

through the children's ears and see through their eyes, where fears and worries may diminish their spiritual development. This may be especially true in the spiritual development of women, who need to know that they are also made in God's image.

Female spirituality has always been concerned with wholeness and connectedness. It continues to be grounded in values that are held to be sacred. We know that goddess worship was common throughout at least thirty thousand years of prehistory. What is most intriguing, however, is that Paleolithic art and artifacts commonly portray women as mothers, and "Venus" figurines from twenty thousand years ago show exaggerated sexual characteristics: full pendulous breasts, enlarged buttocks and pregnant bellies. The earth goddess was above all else fertile, yielding endless cycles of birth and death, populating the earth and providing grains and vegetables to feed its inhabitants. The goddess and the "gynocentric" view has always focused on bringing life and nourishment, and more often than not was also centered on intercommunication and peace.

When the goddesses of earth and moon were replaced by the gods of sky and sun, everything changed. However, the divine image of goddess/mother or mother of the gods was never totally lost to men or women. In a different aspect, Mary the mother of Jesus is venerated by many Christians for her own divine and earthly roles.

There are many interesting books that describe the role of the goddess in Western civilization and about the influence of women on Judeo-

Christianity, but for now suffice it to say that while men were busy codifying doctrines and creeds, women were generally busy "freeing" the spiritual force of life, showing compassion and caring for the plight of others. The Jewish view is that women are inherently more spiritual and therefore are not time-bound in their prayers as are men. Women's strength lies in their deep connection to God. Their spirituality is a part of everything they do, including creating a home.

> *The feminine face of God is an aspect of divinity and an approach to the sacred that is not exclusively of women, but women will naturally lead the way because women's receptivity, commitment to relationships and biological experience provide greater opportunities for this kind of revelation.*
>
> —Jean Shinoda Bolen

Similarly, sexuality, which is present in all of human experience, is surely present in any feminine view of the sacred. Neither males nor females can escape from their bodies, and however much the male-dominated Christian religions have tried to draw a line between body and soul or flesh and spirit, women have a monthly reminder of the futility of such thinking. For women, sexuality is a way of knowing, of connecting the human and the divine in acts of love. Lee J. Richmond has conducted a recent study of women attending class in several Catholic colleges. The women were divided into two groups: women (19–21 years of age) and "older" women (23–62 years of age). The majority of both groups considered themselves to be "almost always" sexual. Interestingly, women of both groups thought that spirituality could exist independently from religion, but not from the body. In another study Gina Ogden had the same findings. For most women sexuality and spirituality are integrated in a whole-person process that connects body, mind and soul. Edwina Gateley, a feminist English lay missionary, calls the God whom women can especially hear, who is felt deep within, "God of the belly button," rather than the more rational God of the head who is separate and far away.

Most women have a longing to live their lives from a deep sacred place of God within themselves, to experience God's presence in the "now." To do this, we as women must love all of ourselves and that includes our bodies. This is perhaps not as easy to do in today's world as it was in the ancient world of full-figured goddesses. Even in medieval and Renaissance art the ideal bodies of women looked amply rounded. Self-esteem enhancer Anita Roddick, founder and chief executive of the Body Shop, has said the following about the body, "There are three billion women in the world who don't look like super models and only eight who do." She has suggested that older women need to help young girls rely on something other than what the media try to feed them about shape and size. In her publication, *Full Voice,* she says, "Cut the suit to fit the body," and not the other way around. We don't have to look like the original "Barbie."

This is critically important for all of us to hear. In terms of body image, adolescent girls from ten different countries rated themselves as having a more negative body image and lower global self-esteem than did boys. This finding of Offer, Ostrov, Howard and Atkinson was reported by Anne Marshall and Marla Avery in the October 1999 issue of the *School Counselor.* Marshall and Avery also reported that adolescent girls, who are more reflective and more engaged in meaning-making than boys, claim that society is sexist because it values physical attractiveness in women above their other attributes.

> *As the body is clad in the cloth, and the flesh in the skin, and the bones in the flesh, and the heart in the whole, so are we, soul and body, clad in the Goodness of God....*
>
> —Juliana of Norwich

Women must not allow the male-dominated media to rob us of the sacred. We can satisfy our spiritual hunger only when we are free to be ourselves, free to "work the earth of the heart" as so aptly stated by Kathleen Norris in her book, *The Cloister Walk.* God of a thousand names. How can we as women know this God? We can trace God as *Echod* (the Hebrew "One"). We know God as *Echod* when we are one with ourselves, one with others in service, and one with the earth, its fields, silos, and windmills.

We can know God as familiar in the faces of friends and family. We can know God as fire, even as did Moses, when we address the fire of our own passion for freedom and peace. Like the mystics throughout time, we can know God as Lover, as Bridegroom and as Bride. As biblically expressed in "I am the Rose of Sharon, the Lily of the Valley," we may see God in spring flowers and wooded mountains.

Perhaps some twenty-first-century women also know God as the one who says *"lekh-lekha"* (go forth) "to the land that I will show you." Go forth to build a new earth community based on social justice where we will see our black and our yellow sons and daughters flourish beside our white children, and we will no longer see our gay children bleed.

"Lekh-lekha!" We hear it as Abraham first heard it. But how do we as mothers and grandmothers give voice to the women who have been abused and who have forgotten how to speak? And how do we who have served for generations let go and let someone do for us? How do we pace ourselves so that our creative spirits bubble forth, and our daydreams find a sacred space in which to receive life and the penetration of self and ideas? How do we strip our lives of old wallpaper, and prune the vines to make room for beauty and new growth?

God of a thousand faces and a thousand names: Savior, Redeemer, Everlasting, Omniscient and All Merciful, walk with us so that each of us can depart from the land of anonymity and find our voice.

HIGHLIGHTS

Bring your WomanSoul to life...

Appreciate your sacred essence...

Nourish your soul...

Recognize the transcendent and live the authentic...

Relate to the Divine Mystery in your own way...

Wear your halo at a jaunty angle...

Appreciate your holy Spirit...

Enjoy the goddess within...

Find your own voice and share it with others...

Birth the Creator in your WomanSoul...

PERSONAL REFLECTIONS

1. Draw a picture that illustrates/describes/depicts your spirituality. (Don't be concerned about whether or not you can draw well. The drawing process is what is important. Remember, you don't need to show this to anyone. It is just for you.)

2. Is your spirituality and your religion the same or different for you? How?

3. In this chapter we say that feminine spirituality has always been concerned with wholeness and connectedness. We also say that for some women, it is difficult to relate to or feel connected to the patriarchal forms in many religions. How does this premise fit for you? Not fit for you? Do you have any places where you can talk with other women about their experiences? Name a few.

4. We speak about "God of a thousand names." What is your name(s) for the Deity? How do you respond to the question: "What can I call you when I talk to you in prayer?"

5. What is prayer for you?

6. In this chapter you read Lee's story and Bev's story and Jean's story about an aspect of their spiritual lives. What is the story you would share about your spiritual life? Perhaps you can write in your journal, your own story a _____'s STORY.

7. Are your spirituality and sexuality connected? In what ways?

8. Finding your voice: What does that mean to you? What helps and what hinders you from finding and speaking out in your voice? Is there a special person who inspires you and helps you find your voice?

What Brings You to Life?

"Laughter"; "Play"

"Envisioning new possibilities"

"Experimentation"

"Helping people to learn new things; learning with them"

"Playing with grandchildren—seeing their smiling faces"

"Finding my heart space"

"A funny movie"

"Joy—it lifts me up"

"Learning to yearn for my own self-care"

"Expressing creativity"

"Gardening; quilting"

"Photography"

"Making things: a challenge"

"My pets: so endearing, so knowledgeable, so much fun"

"Daydreaming; imagining"

"Seeing children's joy in accomplishments"

"Creating something at the sewing machine"

"Pelicans"; "Penguins"; "Puffins and otters"

"Seeing children's faces when they are laughing; tittering; giggling and playing together"

"Doing needlework; yarns of every texture and hue"

What Brings You to Life?

"Being able to laugh"

"Traveling to fascinating places"

"Enjoying children's curious questions, their freedom in play"

"The whole creative process leading to writing a book"

"Rejuvenated by meaningful discussions—interactions and different perspectives on myself"

"Music and moving my body to the flowing patterns"

"A smile and the resonance of truth"

"My spirit flowing free"

6

Discovery, Creativity and Mirth

If I had my life to live over, I would start barefoot
earlier in the spring and stay that way later in the fall.
I would go to more dances. I would ride more merry-go-rounds.
I would pick more daisies.
—Nadine Stair

Suppose that we had started this chapter with the other question that we asked women, "What deadens you?" How would your creative spirit flow free in the face of so much negativity? Read on to hear the many anguished answers, some of which may be your own.

What Deadens You?

"Boredom; repetition; not being creative"

"Negative comments and feelings"

"Unkindness; injustice"

"Intolerance leading to rejection and sadness; ignorance leading to hurt and shame"

"People who are unwilling to change or accept change"

"Finger pointing; faultfinding"

"Abusive people: verbal and physical"

"Burdens of daily life: as paying bills, etc."

"Being ignored; avoided"

"Hypocrisy"

"Disregard for human life"

"Being with a 'stress carrier' who is always complaining"

"A boss who thinks he is the only one in the world who can do anything right"

"Self accusations"

"Lack of appreciation"

"Unpleasant people"

"No matter what I do or say, it's just not good enough"

"Feeling undervalued or unloved"

"Housework—cleaning up messes"

"Angry words and complaints from people"

"Excessive work; overcommitment"

"Policies; politics"

"Pulled in twenty directions"

"Illness and pain"

"Being asked to do one more thing"

"Micromanagers"

"Clutter—even though I create it"

"People who are very judgmental"

"Forced to do an activity"

"Not enough rest, sleep"

"Dullness"

"The junk on television"

"Unhappy people"

"Intentional aggravation by someone;
  unwarranted intrusion"

"Violence of many of our youth today"

"Nonacceptance"

"Disrespect"

"Invalidation of someone due to prejudice"

"People fighting or screaming"

"Negativity: my own and others'"

"Self-centered men and women"

"Intolerance, rigidity"

"People who don't listen"

"Shopping and other mundane chores"

"Overload; superresponsibility"

> *Woman can best refind herself by losing herself in some kind of creative activity of her own.*
> —Anne Morrow Lindbergh

As we've said previously, all the seasons of a woman are what we are; what deadens us is being what we are not.

> *Stay away from critics...people with pursed lips.*
> —Robert J. Wicks

Seeking Your Buried Treasure Within

You choose to say, "Yes!" to exploration and discovery. You are full of anticipation, alive with possibilities. What happens when someone kills your spirit?

BEV'S STORY: *Destiny Denied—Hope Renewed*

One day, while I was studying in my pastoral counseling program, I was having a serious discussion with several of my classmates who were nuns. They were concerned and upset because there were not enough men going into the priesthood and yet women were not allowed to do so. However, the nuns were fulfilling many of the priestly duties and in some of the churches they were the only vowed religious persons available who were serving the congregation. They could do everything except consecrate the bread and wine, celebrate the Mass and administer other sacraments. They named all of the duties that they were allowed to perform as leaders in the parish. I wondered at the time, did someone consider these things too holy for women to do? I had been listening closely to this rather animated and lively discussion, which continued until there was a slight pause. Unlike these women, I was not a nun and yet, I felt compelled to speak for the first time, "Believe me, I know how you feel!"

> *The sense of this word among the Greeks affords the noblest definition of it; enthusiasm signifies "God in us."*
>
> —Germaine de Stael

My classmates looked at me as if I couldn't possibly understand the depth of their feelings. And, yet, I did know. I had been fascinated by what they could and, ultimately, could not do. My whole self was resonating with them as women, and as someone whose former career, knowledge and spirit had been crushed by others in power. I knew what it was like to put so much of myself into a calling, only to have "my hands slapped" and have to step aside at the culminating moment. For, you see, I was a certified nurse-midwife who was prepared to care for a woman throughout her life, to help during the entire labor and delivery and even to assess and care for the infant. However, the actual delivery of the baby was denied to me by doctors, hospitals and the medical insurance climate at the time. The physician that I worked with, Dr. C. Douglas Lord, wanted me to have delivery privileges, and he said that when he had to step in to do the delivery it felt like taking candy from a baby. I had been caring for some of these women for years, had worked hard and bonded so well with them and their families, and then when they were in labor it seemed unfair that I was not allowed to help them bring forth this new life.

There had been such promise for my career, and I remember vividly the day that I learned that I had passed my national certification exam. When I opened the letter, I ran out to the front yard where my husband and son were playing ball, and shouted, "I got my 'C' and now I'm a C.N.M.!" Dave said, "That's great!" Mark, who was only ten, asked, "What does the C stand for?" I paused and then he said, "Oh, I know, caring!"

These were priceless words, especially to a mother, but they also represented a special sense that he had about the other nurse-midwives that he had come to know and the caring that they demonstrated in their work. He knew that we had worked hard to improve the lives of mothers and babies directly and to advance the cause of nurse-midwifery in the legislature.

My career story as well as those of my classmates are not that unusual. As women, we often have difficult choices to make. We can allow others to dictate our destiny, letting them be responsible for crushing our enthusiasm, joy and creativity. Or, we can fight for the rights we believe in. Both Dr. Lord and the doctor who covered for him, Dr. Pablo Renart, were helpful and fought alongside me to make changes.

> *Joy is the holy fire that keeps our purpose warm and our intelligence aglow.*
>
> —Helen Keller

Ultimately, none of us may be able to control circumstances, but our attitude and our perspective are crucial. We can be tripped up by our expectations, and lose hope altogether or we can enjoy the small victories of beauty and joy around us—whether it's the tiny flower pushing through the crack in the rock, or the mother's tears of joy as she beholds her newborn.

It's been hard for me to surrender my expectations. And yet when I do, I'm always amazed at how life surprises me with joy.

—Sarah Ban Breathnach

Fortunately, more and more certified nurse-midwives have hospital and delivery privileges as well as work from free-standing birthing centers, and the statistics related to their care are excellent. They care for the whole person and have compassion for the life that the woman and her family leads as well.

Let Your Senses Soar: All Twelve or More

Do you have a sixth sense? Would you believe that you have twelve senses or more? Most women have a strong intuitive (sixth) sense of perception. Senses are defined as "the power of the mind to know what happens outside itself;...the faculties of the mind or soul;...a feeling; understanding; appreciation." The five senses that are most well known and have specific receptors in the body are of course: hearing, sight, touch, smell and taste. However, what of the many other senses that allow us not only to move through life, but to savor it?

Creativity is close to compassion because both processes are about the making of connections.

—Matthew Fox

Many senses come into play (pun intended) when seeking discovery, creativity and mirth. There is the sense of adventure, a sense of passion as well as compassion, oftentimes common sense and a sense of humor that includes the all-important nonsense.

Imagination is the eye of the soul.

—Joseph Joubert

Maria Cooper Janis says that the way she learned about the world through play and her delight in the nature around her came through her father, actor Gary

Cooper, whose enthusiasm, discipline and love sparked creativity in the whole family.

BEV'S STORY: *A Little Child Leads Us*

A good friend has a grandson named Austin, who, when he was two years old learned a valuable lesson while playing. Someone wanted to play catch with him and he wanted to play catch, too, but he had a toy phone in his hand which he had been playing with quite happily. He looked from the ball to the phone and said, "I can't do both; I have to put this phone away."

> *This was the best school of all—play—*
> *and there was lots of it, together as a family,*
> *part of a bigger thing. It was*
> *part of life—*
> *lessons without being LESSONS.*
> —Maria Cooper Janis

This story also illustrates that we can learn from small children—if we will only observe and listen to them—not only a sense of play, but common sense as well. As women, how often do we try to do two or more things at once, trying to please everyone? Even if it is something enjoyable, we cannot fully appreciate each activity or each person involved.

> *Keep away from the wisdom that does not cry,*
> *the philosophy that does not laugh, and the greatness*
> *that does not bow before children.*
> —Kahlil Gibran

BEV, JEAN AND LEE'S STORY: *Explore Being*

> *Take the trip.*
> *Purchase the gift.*
> *Do it. The seized*
> *opportunity*
> *renders joy.*
> —Max Lucado

Just as we need to be open to the wisdom of children, so can we learn as we mature. All three of us feel that we have a greater sense of adventure since we passed the age of thirty something. We all are willing to try new things and don't worry about perfection, only possibilities. Lee travels a great deal as a speaker and consultant, knows all the airline routes and how to get around in different cities. When she was younger, she was concerned about venturing out in strange cities. Now, she will explore just about anywhere. Lee considers herself a maverick, and Bev resonates with this as well. After all, she says, "I'm a pastoral counselor who had been a nurse-midwife and who really loves to dance." Jean and Lee wanted to know if Bev thought she moved better now than when she was younger, because she has taken so many dance classes in all those years. Bev definitely doesn't think she moves better, but certainly there is more feeling in the movement, especially with sacred dance, which is so inspiring that she feels really connected to her inner self, to her soul. Jean says that she, herself, does many more physical activities now, exercising a great deal and walking around a nearby lake two or three times a week. "When I was forty, I started backpacking, which I think came along with my appreciation of nature and the need to be part of it." At the same time, Jean says that "For me, exploring possibilities is letting myself become more of who I truly am. Rather than being a high achiever as I have been in my thirties and forties, I am learning to do less and listen more to the still small voice of God within. I'm becoming more of a Be-er than a Do-er."

What we're all experiencing is our potential for growth, and this is one of our hopes for the people reading this book. We hope that we are preparing the soil for the seeds of possibilities. There is a capacity in all of us for something great. What can you do better at your age than when you were younger? What is your capacity, not so much the amount, but what makes you different? Part of the answer is letting go of the things we don't need or of fears that we have. We have losses as we age, but the kernel of passion deep

> *You never grow old until you've lost all your marvels.*
>
> —Merry Browne

within each of our hearts can have fire and intensity. Do you sow this seed so that it is life-giving to yourself and others? Some people have that capacity, that inner spark that allows them to sow in good soil, no matter how bad their life is externally. For others, the soil is so depleted that it doesn't appear that the flame can ever be fanned enough to get the spark to fire.

> *There is in every true woman's heart a spark of heavenly fire.*
>
> —Washington Irving

AIMEE'S STORY: *"The Sexiest Thing a Woman Can Have"*

Aimee Mullins says that the sexiest thing a woman can have is confidence—"much sexier than any body part." She has a passion for helping people develop inner strength and beauty, something she knows a great deal about. When she was one year old, both legs had to be amputated below the knee. By age two, she was walking with prostheses and from then on running, biking, skiing and swimming—to name just a few of her athletic activities. At age twenty-two she

> *Aerodynamically the bumblebee shouldn't be able to fly, but the bumblebee doesn't know it so it goes on flying anyway.*
>
> —Mary Kay Ash

holds two world records in the paralympics and she's a fashion model. She's even comfortable wearing minidresses because she wants people to get to know the real her, inside and out. Her mission is "to show the world what it means to be a strong, successful, sexy amputee." Her sense of passion and creativity in the face of what could have been a devastating blow to most young people has led her to cofound HOPE (Helping Other People Excel) which is designed to help athletes with disabilities. She credits her parents and aunts for encouraging her femininity and strength while not coddling or shielding her from the difficulties of life as an amputee.

LEE'S STORY: *I'm Cooking Better in My Mother's Pots*

> *We must have perseverance and above all confidence in ourselves. We must believe that we are gifted for something...*
> —Marie Curie

I never was much of a cook. The first meal I made after I was married was a total disaster. In my desire to please my young husband, I read a cookbook like one reads a chemistry experiment. I remember placing in a pot a little of this and a little of that and called it a stew. I was pleased when I saw the various elements (no pun intended) simmering together.

Then I heard his feet on the stairs. He was coming home. The next thing I realized was that he'd be in the room very soon, and I did so want the stew to be finished when he walked in. The next ingredient to be placed in the pot was flour. I didn't read that flour had to be mixed with something to make a paste before it was to enter the pot with the rest of the ingredients. I took the flour and threw it into the pot; immediately, my stew was filled with small flour mountains, lumps that I could not get rid of. I didn't want my husband to see the stew, the misbegotten stew, and so I threw it in the sink. It stopped up the drain.

In retrospect, I should have known that his anger that night was but a precursor to the divorce that would occur thirty years later. But, all I knew that night was tears, frustration and shame. Eventually, after he unplugged the drain, we went out to dinner together, but my cooking esteem dropped to almost zero, and it was a long time before I tried a stew again.

However, fifteen years later, I was chair of the social science division of a community college, and I decided to have a party for all the people in my division. There were fourteen of us, and the party was scheduled for February 14, Valentine's Day. My secretary, who was also my friend, asked me who was going to cook for the party. She knew me well enough to know that I had few skills in that area. However, I told her that I wanted to cook for the party. She simply said, "Oh," and let the matter drop.

Three days before the party, I still had no menu. I spoke to my secretary who, by the way, was a gourmet cook. "Jan," I said, "I can't do this!" She replied, "Okay, I'll do it for you." What seemed so difficult for me was so easy for her. It took her less than five minutes to pull a menu together. I approved it wholeheartedly. She said that she would get the food, prepare it, and bring it to my house.

On the day of the party, it snowed and was extremely cold. She brought the food and also several of what looked like Bunsen burners, which I later learned were called chafing dishes. It didn't take her long before she set up a whole catering outfit in my kitchen. I felt helpless. "Jan," I said, "I've got to do this. I've got to help." She told me that I did big and important things and to go upstairs and write some papers, or prepare my next lecture. "Jan," I shook her, "You don't understand, I've got to help." By this time my cooking esteem had actually reached zero. She said, "Okay, help if you must, but I really can do this myself." "Jan," I shouted, "This isn't about you; it's about me. I have to help." "Well, if you must, she said, "Take the cheese spread in the jar over there and put

115

it on some bread; we're making hors d'oeuvres. After you put it on the bread, I'll toast it." I took a knife—the cheese had hardened from the cold. Whatever my IQ should have been, it was absent that day. I took the knife, put it in the cold cheese, and tried to spread the cheese on the bread. The bread tore; I cried. "I'm helpless," I shouted. "No, you're not," said my friend, Jan. "You go upstairs and do the big important things that you do well; I'll do the preparations here." "No," I shouted again, this time even louder. "Don't you understand that I have to do this? My whole self-concept is at stake." Finally, she relented, sighed, and said, "Okay, if you must do it, either heat the cheese or heat the knife."

Mistakes are often the garments in which miracles are cloaked.

—Yitta Halberstam and Judith Leventhal

I know now that my IQ is above average, but that day, I felt less than stupid. However, when she gave me the clue, I was able to run hot water on the knife, quickly wipe the knife, and spread the cheese on the bread. It felt so good. I had learned a competency and, although not yet a cook, I was willing to try again.

Yet, my real cooking breakthrough came later. When my mother died, I inherited the pot that she used to roast meat in. Everyone in the family loved my mother's roasts, and I thought she had a recipe that was something very special. When I had asked my mother how she made her roast, she told me that she just put it in the pot, seasoned it slightly, cooked it, and later threw in a few vegetables like carrots and potatoes with the beef.

When I inherited my mother's pot, which I highly coveted, I truly believed that the pot would help me. And so, I brought it home and tried to cook a roast in that pot. Lo and behold, the roast was delicious. A little later, I cooked a turkey, which was also delicious. I became convinced that my mother's pot was a magic pot, but whether it was or not, it was mystical for me.

Thus, I began cooking for my family every Thanksgiving and every Christmas, but always in my mother's pot.

A Related Story from Grace:

Grace recently came upon a kettle belonging to her mother and was surprised at the deep stirring (no pun intended) of memories it evoked. Not only for the good food that was cooked in it, but for the connections to a very important change that was occurring in their lives when she was a child. Her father was building their house in a nearby town and spent all of his evenings, weekends and vacations doing so. It was a family project, so Grace learned quite a few building skills. However, she also had the important task of bringing a hot supper to her Dad in (you guessed it) the kettle. Her mother packed it and Grace went by trolley and then up a long dirt road to deliver her precious package. Later, when they moved into a couple of rooms with a roof over them, her mother cooked over an outside fire placed between two cement blocks with the top of an oil drum for a cover. The kettle and her small coffeepot had places of honor on this homemade stove. Now, Grace is hoping that she, too, will be cooking better in her mother's kettle.

BEV, JEAN AND LEE'S STORY: *Finding a Mattress That Fits You*

There was much humor, including outright giggling at times as we three authors discussed and developed the themes for this book. We often taped the sessions so that we could speak freely and describe our ideas and feelings. We then became concerned about the secretary who was typing up the notes from the tape. It had to sound confusing because sometimes we laughed over a word or turn of a phrase or we all spoke at once. All three of us like to play with words and we came up with some funny combinations, some of which come across in these pages and some you may be able to imagine for yourself.

We got to talking about bed sizes and mattresses. We decided that you have much more connection in a queen-size bed than in a king-size bed; bigger is not necessarily better. Well, after all, connection is one of the major themes of our book! And, what about mattresses? Jean said that at one time she had a waterbed. Somebody had told her it would be wonderful. She got in and it felt like she was really floating on something and she thought it was terrible. The worst part of the waterbed is that she likes to sit in bed with her books all around her, and the books were moving; everything was moving. So, getting the bed you want is really important, especially the mattress. Lee also has a bed story. She said that she has a mattress that no one else would like because it has no springs. Because of a back problem, she knew that sleeping on a hard surface, even a floor, was beneficial. This mattress is practically like wood and with another mattress on top of it, her back loves the firmness of it.

Are we obsessed about beds and mattresses or what? It would seem that way, but after all this is where people spend much of their lives. Some people spend as much as twelve hours on their mattresses every day, though most people are lucky to have eight hours. Getting a bed that fits you is important, though it may take a long time to find the right one—so too, you've got to find the work that fits you. At this point Jean and Bev asked Lee, "Who is typing this from the tape? She's going to say this is getting more interesting all the time!" and she may even add, "These ladies had wine for lunch." Lee said, "June is typing this." So, we all said, "Hi, June!"

> *Humor isn't for everyone—only for people who want to have fun, enjoy life, and feel alive.*
>
> —Ann Wilson Schaef

Discovery, Creativity and Mirth

We've spent a long time talking about what fits, but that really is a crucial concept. We need to see how the world fits us or how we fit into the world. Lee just had some expensive loafers resoled. The shoemaker thought she was crazy because they have been stitched many times, and in many places, but it took her a long time to find shoes that were so comfortable. "They're broken in, just like the mattress that fits me," she explained to Bev and Jean.

Resoling obviously has its place, but what about "re-souling"? We need to strengthen our inner selves by remembering what brings us to life. For Lee, it is enjoying her ten grandchildren and the theater. We need to find the spirituality that fits us, a way for our souls to shine with the radiance of love for ourselves and others. Bev moves through inspiration in sacred dance, while Jean is nourished by retreats. We each need to find our own path of enlightenment.

We have spoken of shoes and spirituality and mattresses and work—and how they connect. Now, you have a sense of how we played while writing this book. In many ways, it comes down to our having to re-soul ourselves—rejuvenate our souls. Laughter allows us to play and to have heart-fire and soul-shimmer!

Laughter is a freeing dance, performed within the soul.

—Serene West

Be open to *all* of your senses for discovery, creativity and mirth!

119

HIGHLIGHTS

Seek your buried treasure within...

Explore and discover the possibilities...

Release yourself from the prison that binds you...

Enjoy the small wonders...

Let the sacred unfold within you...

Use all twelve of your senses...

Learn from small children...

Sow the life-giving seeds...

Associate with people who make you laugh...

Cultivate your sense of adventure...

Let your daydreams weave spells of enchantment...

Fly kites and blow up more balloons...

Let your soul shimmer...

PERSONAL REFLECTIONS

1. We say in this chapter that there is a capacity in all of us for greatness. What can you do better, or with a richer essence, at your age now than when you were younger?

2. Sometimes, in order to move forward, we need to let go of things or fears that we don't need. What are some remnants of the past that you need to give away or let go of?

3. What helps to re-soul yourself—rejuvenate your soul?

4. What is the kernel of passion deep within your heart that flames with fire and intensity? How do you sow this seed so it is life-giving to yourself and others?

5. A short "quiz" about joy!

- When was the last time you truly laughed—that "deep in your belly" kind of laughter?

- What helps this wellspring of joy and mirth bubble up in you?

- What do you need to do right now to help bring more laughter into your life?

- Who do you need to be with to help you laugh?

- What activities bring out the lighthearted parts of you?

- Can you give yourself a laughter break today instead of a coffee break?

- When you enter a video store, do you hurry to the section marked comedy?

- From whom do you catch joy?

6. List all the ways in which you are creative. Don't let your thoughts of creativity be limited to writing, music or art. Your forms of creativity may be very different—see what "fits" you. (It may be baking a pie, or planting a flower garden, or giving a speech, or crocheting an afghan, or writing a thank-you note, or creating a software program, or drawing out quiet, shy people into meaningful conversation, or soothing a sad child.) Remember that creativity comes in many forms. Celebrate your creativity!

What Brings You to Life?

"Helping students who are caring for people in the community"

"Traveling–exploring new worlds and customs"

"Having balance in my life"

"Working a shift in acute care"

"My garden: beautifying a corner of the world"

"My grandchildren"

"Donna's eye for beauty and the art and creativity she shares
    with others"

"Helping to build a Habitat for Humanity home"

"Traditional stories"

"Sunrises and rainbows"

"Children: the hope and promise of the future and how we must
    treat them carefully"

"Finding my son whom I had given up for adoption and knowing
    he forgives me–he understands"

"Hearing similar hopes and dreams from women in
    the wider world"

"Being in nature lets me know there's something
    greater than myself"

"Feeling closer to God in the woodlands than in
    church"

"Whales around the world"

What Brings You to Life?

"Interconnectedness: hummingbird in South America that is the only one who has a bill that can fertilize a certain flower"

"Learning for a lifetime"

"Having the confidence to follow my dreams"

7

Hope and Healing
in the Wider World

O God, take our tiny acorns of service
and turn them into towering oak trees of hope.
—Marian Wright Edelman

Our Hopeful Healing

Bringing yourSelf to life is the hopeful beginning of healing not only within, but for others as well. The birthing of WomanSoul involves self, God, and others with whom we form relationships and become community. And that community can spread to the wider world. For the healing that begins with yourSelf does not need to end there. Even a young girl, Anne Frank, wrote in her diary that happiness is contagious and that the person who has courage and faith will never perish in misery.

CELINE'S STORY: *The Melody Lingers On*

Glamorous and personable and gifted with a voice that stirs hearts around the world, Celine Dion has been one of Quebec's most noted ambassadors. Indeed, she has brought joy to many people.

Though her voice and melody will linger on, she has chosen to walk away from world tours and recording in order to concentrate on being home with her husband and starting their family. She has always loved being home with her family and friends and has special relationships with her siblings' and friends' children. Celine has begun to spread that happiness with a child of her own.

> *...the very least you can do in your life is to figure out what you hope for. And the most you can do is live inside that hope. Not admire it from a distance but live right in it, under its roof.*
>
> —Barbara Kingsolver

People who bring healing and hope to others are not necessarily gorgeous or physically fit. The world would be in really big trouble if these were the qualifications. Of course some of the "beautiful people" do give much of their time, talents and money to significantly help others. However, it is often the special saints who know sorrow and heartache firsthand that are able to understand the needs of vulnerable people.

PEEP'S STORY: *Let's Hope You Don't Have to Be Gorgeous*

Life magazine had an article in the June, 1991 issue titled, "So This Is What a Saint Looks Like..." At seventy years of age, and only four feet ten inches tall, Fanniedell Peeples (affectionately known as Peep) is a tower of strength and comfort to many people. Her radiant smile belies her many ills and misshapen body, with a crooked spine and bony hump over her right shoulder. She is the hub and heart of a children's hospital surgical waiting room, where anxious friends and family gather for word of the young patients having surgery. She dispenses humor and common sense, holds hands and imparts soothing words or a pep talk as appropriate. She is able to give of herself to others even though her life has not been an easy one. Her mother died soon after her birth and her father lived only a few more years. She was taunted because of her outer appearance and she learned to allow her beautiful inner self to shine forth. She became an inspiration to others and continues to amaze people. She has won awards and honors, but is happiest working with babies and children. Despite her pain which is a constant companion, she is very active, but also knows when her body needs to rest. Her life is a wonderful example of healing oneself while giving hope to others.

> I have never been especially impressed by the heroics of the people convinced that they are about to change the world. I am more awed by the heroism of those who are willing to struggle to make one small difference after another.
>
> —Ellen Goodman

> Every painful event contains in itself a seed of growth and liberation.
>
> —John Welch

JONI'S STORY: *The World Needs More Wheels*

Joni's story of pain and loss has culminated in the worldwide network, Wheels for the World. In 1967, when she was a robust teenager, Joni Eareckson (now Tada) had a severe diving accident that left her a quadriplegic.

129

After many struggles, including an even more crippling depression result-ing from the dramatic changes in her life, she began to reach out with hope through her Christian ministries to the community of people with disabilities. One fascinating project begun in recent years demonstrates her creativity as well as the depth of her commitment to the community at large. Wheels for the World is an international program designed to send refurbished wheelchairs to areas of the world where there is a great need but few resources. She has reached out to other segments of the community who are also in great need. Under the guidance of mechanically minded senior citizens, prisoners have volunteered to refurbish 1,500 wheelchairs annually, which are sent to developing coun-tries through Hope Haven International Ministries. The prisoners benefit greatly not just by learning job skills, but in knowing that their work has meaning, that they are making a significant difference in many people's lives. She recently wrote, "Like butterflies breaking free from outgrown cocoons, disabled people worldwide are joyfully and fully participating in life, carried on the wings of a new wheelchair."

> *My wheelchair is the prison*
> *God has used to set my spirit free!*
> —Joni Eareckson Tada

Joni has moved beyond the confines of her wheelchair, which indeed could seem like a prison. By gifting others with their own wheelchairs worldwide she has freed many who are incapacitated. At the same time, she is freeing the minds, hands and hearts of prisoners (who are behind prison walls) to become part of a worldwide service. And, that is only one of her ministries. What a calling!

MINNIE'S STORY: *A Wider World, A Bigger Net*

Minnie was in her eighties and ill when her family traveled back to her homeland. She had planned to go, but her doctor thought it unwise. She was very disappointed, but her daughter thought of a wonderful plan. She and her family set up a Web site so that Minnie could travel along with her family through the messages and pictures sent to her each day on her computer. With the help of friends to get her started, Minnie was soon able to send messages back and discuss all that she was seeing and hearing about in her family's travelogue. It was the next best thing to being there. Here is technology at its best—a new way for a caring community to free those who need to be transported beyond the confines of their restricted lives.

Pass It On, Pass It On

How do we learn to rise above our adversities and to help others? Marian Wright Edelman is a champion for children in both the political and community arenas. She is the founder of the Children's Defense Fund and, as she states, "I do what I do because my parents did what they did and were who they were." She sees them as having "integrity, consistency, common sense, high expectations, study, service and play, sacrifice and bedrock faith." She feels that parents should be mentors to their children so that when times are difficult for them, the children will have remembered strength on which to draw. We never know what a child will remember that may have a vital impact later in his or her life.

BEV'S STORY: *Quietly behind the Scenes*

In 1903, my mother was born with rickets (a calcium loss from vitamin D deficiency that causes softening of the bones, with associated skeletal deformities). She didn't walk until she was seven years old, and in the meantime her brothers and sisters carried her around on a board so that she could go wherever they went to play. Perhaps it was life from this perspective that made her sensitive to the needs of those less fortunate: the handicapped, the poor and the uneducated.

Sharing my clothes and toys with the needy was an early lesson, even though my own clothes were usually made by my mother from "hand-me-downs."

> We are cups constantly and quietly being filled. The trick is knowing how to tip ourselves over and let the beautiful stuff out.
>
> —Ray Bradbury

Often, I would mention a child at school who was having problems. One such boy was taunted by everyone in the class for being "so stupid." Frank (not his real name) didn't really seem stupid to me, but he did seem to be having trouble catching on to the work in the class. His parents, from eastern Europe, had not been in the United States very long and I wondered if he was just having difficulty with English. He wore very thick glasses that made the kids laugh even more. When I talked with him, he just smiled and said very little. He sat at the back of the room, and since his eyesight was already corrected, I wondered if he was able to hear the assignments.

Upon hearing this story, my mother took me to visit him at his home. His family was so glad to have visitors because they were very lonely in this country. His mother had been worried about Frank having a hearing problem, but she didn't know how to have it tested. My mother must have gone to the school shortly after this conversation, because soon Frank was seated in the front row and a few weeks later had been fitted with a hearing aid. His comprehension improved rapidly. My parents probably donated money toward his hearing aid, but they never spoke of it. I learned later that they had been helping people long before I was born.

They had helped to send a young niece to college even though their own resources were meager following the Great Depression. For two years around that same time, my mother took in and cared for a small child in the neighborhood whose mother was gravely ill. There was no thought about any monetary reward. Years later, I noticed that one of my classmates was very poorly dressed and I mentioned it to Mom. Eloise (not her real name) was also unkempt and was teased by her classmates because of it. My mother must have rallied several mothers together, for Eloise soon started appearing in nicer clothes. One day, I even recognized one of my favorite outfits that my mother had made for me, but of course I said nothing. The expression on Eloise's face was pure joy, and it was more than matched by my inner glow.

There are other stories of quiet caring behind the scenes, many of which I will never know, but the lessons linger, as does the joy that my mother brought to me and others.

> *To love is to receive a glimpse of heaven.*
> –Karen Sunde

Whether we work in our own small corner of the world, or we have the opportunity to spread the net of compassion worldwide, our personal hope will come from being involved in a community of caring. Think of the communities in which you may act with compassion: family, friends, neighbors, school, work, religious organizations, charities and other volunteer organizations. There are many avenues by which to bring hope and healing to others. However, becoming involved presumes that you are first taking care of that special community within yourSelf. There is an intricate system of checks and balances among your cells and synapses, your tissues, your emotions and your soul-filled yearnings. These components require hearty laughter, soothing thoughts, creativity and play and delicate fine tuning.

We cannot take the idea of balance too lightly. Some of the facts relating to the demands on women's time is nothing short of daunting, perhaps even haunting. In mid-1990, *Newsweek* reported that "the average American woman will spend 17 years raising children and 18 years helping aged parents." Some women may have both sets of responsibilities at

> *My family is like this old sweater—it keeps unraveling, but then someone figures out how to sew it up one more time; it has lumps and then it unravels again, but you can still wear it; and it still keeps away the chill.*
>
> —Anne Lamott

the same time, while other women may also be caring for grandchildren on a full-time basis. Even when sharing the responsibilities, many women also have work outside the home that is demanding of their time. It's exhausting to think of the sheer energy level needed to perform these various tasks and still maintain a caring presence. Women in these circumstances really need "respite care," which means that someone else comes in and takes over the care for a specified time so that she and perhaps the family can have some time away to relax and catch their collective breaths. If you are in this type of caregiving circumstance, please be sure to give yourSelf a break.

When it comes to balance, each woman must find her own. Picture a circle with the following words at the periphery: *work, friendship, learning, spirituality, leisure, family* and *citizen*. These words stand for things that we do and are, and how we spend our time. Now, picture yourself at

> *The universe, like a bellows, is always emptying, always full. The more it yields, the more it holds.*
>
> —Tao-te Ching

the center of the circle, facing in turn each word at the periphery. If the periphery is a ten and the center is a zero, imagine how much time you spend in each area of your life and draw a line from the center

whose length corresponds to the extent of your involvement in that area. Then, connect the lines. To illustrate, look at the circle that follows. We will call this one *Joyce's Circle.*

Joyce's Circle

Although Joyce's diagram does not look balanced (Joyce spends a lot of time with work and family, less on leisure and still less as a citizen), she says that she feels balanced. She feels that her work is fun.

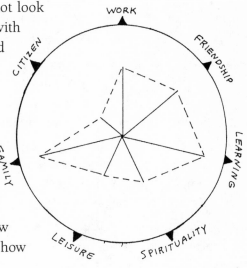

Now, you may want to fill in your diagram that reflects how much time you spend in the areas of friendship, learning, spirituality, leisure, family, citizen and work. Remember that it is based on how much time you currently spend, not how much you think you ought to spend.

_____'s Circle

As you look at your diagram, do you feel balanced? If not, what might you change? Do what you need to do in order to balance and replenish yourSelf, remembering that needs change in life. Balance is like a seesaw. You have to be flexible and continuously readjust your position to live life fully in a healthy and hopeful way.

Three important ingredients needed for balance and healing are laughter, love and peace. Norman Cousins, author of *Anatomy of*

135

> *If you can't make it better, you can laugh at it.*
>
> —Erma Bombeck

an Illness, popularized the concept that laughter releases endorphins that are measurable in our blood and yield a sense of euphoria and happiness that are healing to body and soul and give us peace. Our lives are enriched when we find people who exemplify these ingredients.

Rosalynn Carter and her husband, former President Jimmy Carter, are just such models of love, laughter and peace. Instead of retiring to the presidential library, the Carters have given the people of Georgia and the wider world two great gifts in addition to his peace initiatives: Habitat for Humanity and a National Symposium on Mental Illness. With the first gift, which also involves a national fund-raising effort, the Carters construct homes for the poor, and with the second gift they help mental health workers reconstruct lives.

> *The common tasks are beautiful if we have eyes to see their shining ministry.*
>
> —Grace Noll Crowell

Mrs. Carter has been involved with the cause of mental health since her days in the White House. It is she who plans programs and discusses issues with mental health professionals. Several years ago, at a dinner held for the participants of the symposium, Mr. Carter laughingly told the people at his table how he often was out boiling peanuts for the group to eat after Mrs. Carter finished talking with physicians about their joint work in mental health. He thought the juxtaposition of their roles delightfully funny, especially his small but tasty contribution to the table—laughter turned to love brings joy and healing.

We are all interrelated and therefore must take care to preserve and not destroy the resources God has given to us, whether it be people or the environment. Loving hands have crafted and planted, sewn and sown. It's crucial to teach children to appreciate the many ways that resources can be utilized and admired. We saw a beautiful example at Jean's home in the form of a lovely quilted angel. Someone many years ago had lovingly made a quilt that had become worn from much use and many washings. Now it was being resurrected with wings and a heart: re-souled and still treasured, but now in a different metaphor.

> *Perhaps what we are called to do may not seem like much, but the butterfly is a small creature to affect galaxies thousands of light years away.*
>
> —Madeleine L'Engle

Another illustration of preserving resources, love and laughter is a story of the Blank brothers. As jobbers they bought odd lots of merchandise and sold the goods in their retail store. One year, close to Easter time, one of the brothers bought a "lot" of paint—part in light pink, the rest in green— as well as some material to make plaster. Another brother bought small flower pots. None of these items sold. But, one day one of the brothers got an idea. He mixed the paints into the plaster and poured the plaster into the flower pots. As the plaster was becoming firm, into each pot he then placed cloth flowers, of which he had many and which also were not selling in

> *Light tomorrow with today!*
>
> —Elizabeth Barrett Browning

their retail store. The brothers then placed the potted flowers out in the store for Easter and Mother's Day sales. They sold them to people in the neighborhood for ten cents so that even children could purchase them. The outcome was that they couldn't sell enough of them. They had to go out for more paint, more flowers, more plaster and more pots. Now, the children had gifts for their mothers who greatly appreciated such a pretty and clever idea. Easter dinner tables sprouted these special centerpieces and traffic in the store increased incrementally.

Add laughter and love to Self, make something out of seemingly nothing, and the result is a sense of wellness, a sense of balance that comes from making the world a little bit better place.

> *Women's work is always toward wholeness.*
>
> —May Sarton

Ultimately what we need for healing and hope is faith—in God, in others and in ourselves as women. In a world based on logic and positivism, faith is not easy because it embraces mystery and unknowing. We have to work to be comfortable with unknowing. We are so used to worshiping the known: "the three A's—achievement, affluence and appearance" as stated by Marcus Borg. But these things can deaden us. Faith says that we can be beautiful at eighty...that wrinkles hold more hope than a twenty-two-inch waistline. Faith knows that we can be blessed when poor because we can then be open to all possibilities, and faith also knows that all achievement is fleeting. Mystery remains. As women we need to have faith in the future, faith in our children and in our ability to raise them and faith that even unbidden, God is present with us in the endeavor.

In the Jewish religion, girls at the age of thirteen become bat mitzvah and boys become bar mitzvah. These "daughters" and "sons of the blessing" read to an assembly of people from the Torah. Generally after the readings, the girl or boy gives a speech. The following was given by Bryan Wexler, age thirteen, as part of his bar mitzvah speech.

"I would like to talk about a very special person in my life. Someone who taught me by example to choose life: Margie Downs. She was my grandmother's best friend, and she was a good friend to my family. Margie's mother was Jewish, but she was raised Catholic and became a nun. We would visit with her all the time. Margie was the type of person that you loved to be around. I thought about her a lot and would always look forward to seeing her. Whenever we were with her it was magical. She made me laugh, she made me smile. She would come to my grandmom's house for Thanksgiving, Chanukah, Passover, birthdays or other special occasions. She would also come over to just have fun and to be with my family. Margie was loving and caring and very nice. She was encouraging and helpful and she was truly a wonderful person.

"She had a favorite saying, which is now my philosophy about life, 'Choose Life.' This statement comes from Devarim-Deuteronomy 30:19: 'I call heaven and earth to record this day against you, that I have set before you life and death, blessing and cursing; therefore choose life, that both you and your seed may live.'

"I think this saying makes a lot of sense. From this we learn that we have free will. Margie definitely chose life, maybe more than anyone I know. She was always happy and she always looked on the bright side. Margie had cancer complicated by hepatitis C, but even when she was sick she was loving. Margie was always thinking of others. I am honored to have been such good friends with her. She was truly a great person and I miss her so much!

Life shrinks or expands in proportion to one's courage.

—Anais Nin

"...I am trying to tell you today, 'To everything there is a season, and a time to every purpose under heaven' [Ecclesiastes 3:1]. Enjoy life, this is not a dress rehearsal. Amen."

HIGHLIGHTS

Balance the system within yourSelf first and keep your life simpler...

Accept comforting and care...

Share your gifts and spread your joy...

Laugh often with others for your benefit, too...

Do small acts lovingly—they can have great impact...

Let your spirit fly free from the chains that bind your body and mind...

Pass on the caring learned from your parents and mentors...

Artfully resurrect worn treasures into new—preserve resources...

Make the world a little bit better place as you pass through...

Be proud of your wrinkles, especially if they are "laugh crinkles"...

...in a time lacking
in truth and certainty
and filled with anguish and despair,
no woman should be shamefaced
in attempting to give back to the world,
through her work, a portion of its lost heart.

—Louise Bogan

Appear magical in children's eyes...

Live to your fullest for yourSelf and those around you...

PERSONAL REFLECTIONS

1. How do you pass on hope and healing in the wider world? Where are the communities of caring in your life? Where are the places in which you act with compassion to help bring hope and healing to others as you move along on your own healing journey?

2. Often when we think about healing in the wider world, we make the mistake of thinking we need to be doing something "big" to have it be of value. There is a beautiful quote attributed to Mother Teresa regarding God's desires for us, "We can do no great things, only small things with great love." What "small thing with great love" is God asking of you?

3. Sometimes being a healer is as simple as learning how to truly listen and be with another. Elizabeth O'Conner writes in *Cry Pain, Cry Hope,* "I know that there is no more important service in all the world than listening. We cannot be healed until we are listened to, and we cannot be healers until we know how to listen." Who are the people in your life who truly listen to you? Who are the people for whom you can be a healing, listening presence?

4. Three important ingredients for balance and healing are laughter, love and peace. In the last chapter we focused more on the importance of laughter; now we will focus more on love and peace. Where do you experience love in your life? Where do you experience peace? Is there enough love and peace in your life? How could you receive more, and how could you give more love and peace?

5. In the famous Old Testament scripture (Deut 30:19), it says, "Choose life so that you and your descendants may live." Look at the tools listed in the epilogue that help you choose life. Are there some other tools that you would like to add? Begin by choosing one. Follow it. Choose life!

Epilogue

We hope that you are ready to choose life, to choose what brings you to life! We found that people need tools for living in this life-giving manner, and we want to share what others shared with us.

- Be around people who bring you to life: counselors who bring out your creative aspects; people who can hold you when you cry. What deadens is being told you can't cry.

- Breathe deeply and live from the inside out. What deadens is being afraid to breathe or speak.

- Eat great food, especially when you don't have to cook it: almost anything chocolate—especially dark chocolate, honey, biscuits, butterscotch...pink cotton candy, champagne. What deadens is cold french fries.

- Clothing: seek practical sensuality—warmth, textures, beautiful patterns; flannel-lined silk pajamas; a large square of sensuous Indonesian silk. What deadens is wearing things that "scar" you, like pantyhose, underwire bras and clothes that don't keep you warm.

- Find a special place to live, a place that fits your lifestyle, with beautiful things to look at. It may be a cottage surrounded by water or trees, or a house in a cozy neighborhood, or a comfortable, one-level home that accommodates a disability. You should have a good feeling about your home. What deadens is large houses on postage-stamp lots or no house at all.

- Soul play, whimsy and love. What deadens is being told how to believe and how to care.

- Knowing what you want right now; doing what you need right now; living in the moment. What deadens is the fear to move or speak, to feel insecure or inadequate, to have intrusions into your privacy or to feel constraints on your needed time and space.

> *By having reverence for life, we enter into a spiritual relation with the world.*
>
> —Albert Schweitzer

In order to bring yourSelf to life, be aware of the universal languages all around you: laughter, smiles, music and rocking a baby are just a few. When you find new ones for yourSelf, share them with others to expand your own universe and theirs as well.

Let your heart glow and your soul shimmer!

Notes

(All biblical references cited in the text are from the Revised Standard Version unless otherwise noted.)

Prologue
Page 1. Kathleen Fischer, *Autumn Gospel* (Mahwah, N.J.: Paulist Press, 1995), 10.

Page 2. Albert Einstein, quoted in "My Own Life Is Proof," Dan Wakefield, *Guideposts*, March 1996, 2.

Chapter 1. Dancing to the Rhythms of Life
Page 7. Saidie Patterson, quoted in *Soul Weavings: A gathering of Women's Prayers*, Klug, ed. 132.

Isadora Duncan, quoted in "A Celebration of the Spiritual Where Some See Sin," Jennifer Dunning, *New York Times*, Sunday, November 15, 1998, 12.

Page 8. Stanley Plog, quoted in Jim Patterson's "Why Do We Seek the Shore?" *USA Weekend*, June 19–21, 1998, 16.

Page 10. Helen Keller, quoted in *Giving is Caring Page-A-Day Calendar*, Milton Murray, director (Washington, D.C.: Philanthropic Service for Institutions), entry for August 12, 1989.

Page 11. Gene Kelly The source of this quote is unknown.

Quoted in the television series *Joseph Campbell and the Power of Myth*, "The Hero's Adventure," program 1 with Bill Moyers (New York: Mystic Fire Video, Inc., 1988).

Spoken by Mr. Miyagi in *The Next Karate Kid* (Culver City, Calif.: Columbia Pictures Industries [Columbia Tri Star Home Video]), 1994.

Page 12. Matthew Fox, *A Spirituality Named Compassion* (Harper-SanFrancisco, 1990), 131.

St. Teresa of Avila. The source of this quote is unknown.

Page 14. Barbara Johnson, *Living Somewhere Between Estrogen and Death* (Dallas: Word Publishing, 1997), 125.

Dolly Parton, quoted in *Quotable Women of the Twentieth Century*, Tracy Quinn, ed. (New York: William Morrow, 1999), 168.

Page 18. Buffa Hargett, quoted in Joan Leotta, "Even at Three, Children Can Dance, Too, *Montgomery Journal,* December 16, 1983, B1, B10.

Ann Richards, quoted in Patricia O'Gorman, *Dancing Backwards in High Heels: How Women Master the Art of Resilience* (Center City, Minn.: Hazelden, 1994), 1.

Erma Bombeck, *Forever Erma: Best-Loved Writing from America's Favorite Humorist* (Kansas City, Mo.: Andrews McMeel Publishing, 1997), 232.

American Orthopaedic Foot and Ankle Society survey quoted in Carrie St. Michel, "High-Heel Amnesia, Pain? What Pain?" *Good Housekeeping* magazine, March 1998, 176.

Susan Okie, "Shoes that Hurt Women...And the Women Who Love Them," *Washington Post*, Health Sections May 12, 1998, 12.

Page 19. Gilda Radner, quoted in Quinn, *Quotable Women of the Twentieth Century,* 137.

Chapter 2. Connection Is Everything
Page 25. George Eliot (Marian Evans), quoted in *Many Strong and Beautiful Women*, undated engagement calendar (Yellow Springs, Ohio: Antioch Publishing Company, 1994), 63.

Notes

William James. The source of this quote is unknown.

Page 26. Carol Kruckeberg, *What Was Good About Today* (Seattle: Madrona Publishers, 1984), cited in the Reader's Digest Condensed Books (Pleasantville, New York, vol.1, 1990), 158.

Page 27. Eleanor Roosevelt quoted in Armond Eisen's *Friends Forever: A Book of Quotations*, Peggy Bresnick, ed. (Kansas City: Andrews McMeel Publishing, 1997), 323.

Abraham Lincoln, quoted in Eisen, *Friends Forever*, 324.

Mary Breckenridge, *Wide Neighborhoods: A Story of the Frontier Nursing Service* (Lexington: University Press of Kentucky, 1981), 109.

Page 28. George Aschenbrenner, "A Hidden Self Grown Strong," in *Handbook of Spirituality for Ministers,* R. J. Wicks, ed. (Mahwah, N.J.: Paulist Press, 1995), 231.

Page 31. Marge Piercy, quoted in Madeleine L'Engle and Luci Shaw, *Friends for the Journey* (Ann Arbor: Vine Books, Servant Publications, 1997), 13.

Page 32. Madeleine L'Engle, ibid, 46.

Page 34. Unpublished data, Bureau of Labor Statistics, Division of Labor Force Statistics, United States Department of Labor (1999).

Luci Shaw, quoted in L'Engle and Shaw, *Friends for the Journey*, 19.

Page 35. Martin Luther King, Jr., quoted in *Guideposts,* March 2000, back cover.

Page 36. Clement of Alexandria. The source of this quote is unknown.

Page 37. St. Thérèse of Lisieux, quoted in Kathleen Norris, *The Cloister Walk* (New York: Riverhead Books 1997), 27.

Page 38. Julian of Norwich quoted in Klug, *Soul Weaving: A Gathering of Women's Prayers*, 20.

Chapter 3. Valuing Your True Essence along the Journey

Page 47. Marion Woodman with Jill Mellick, *Coming Home to Myself: Reflections for Nurturing a Woman's Body and Soul* (Berkeley, Calif.: Conari Press, 1998), 98.

Page 48. Itzhak Perlman in WETA program, *Great Performances: Itzhak Perlman,* December 27, 1997.

Page 49. Viktor Frankl, *Man's Search for Meaning* (New York: Simon and Schuster, 1959), 108–18, originally published in Austria, 1946.

Allan K. Chalmers, quoted in Mary Engelbreit's *Just for Today, Be Happy 2000 Calendar* (Kansas City: Andrews McMeal Publishing), entry for January 5, 2000.

Page 51. Eleanor Roosevelt, quoted in *Guideposts,* December 1999, 29.

Page 52. Edgar Schein, *Career Anchors: Discovering Your Real Values* (San Diego: Pfeiffer, 1990), 20–32.

Page 54. Kahlil Gibran, *The Prophet* (New York: Alfred A. Knopf, 1964), 28.

John Holland, *Making Vocational Choices: A Theory of Vocational Personalities and Work Environments,* 3rd ed. (Odessa, Fla.: Psychological Assessment Resources, 1997), 21–31.

Angela Morgan, quoted in *Giving Is Caring Page-A-Day Calendar,* entry for September 4, 1989.

Page 55. John Holland, in Edwin L. Herr and Stanley H. Cramer, *Career Guidance and Counseling Through the Lifespan,* 5th ed. (New York: HarperCollins, 1996), 220–221.

John Holland, *Self-Directed Search,* assessment booklet (Form R) (Odessa, Fla.: Psychological Assessment Resources, 1990).

Richard Nelson Bolles, *The 1999 What Color Is Your Parachute?* (Berkeley, Calif.: Ten Speed Press, 1999), 289–90.

Page 57. Anne de Lenclos, quoted in Alexandra Stoddard, *Mothers: A Celebration* (New York: Avon Books, 1996), 114.

Page 58. Jeanne Marie Laskas, quoted in "What She Sowed," *Washington Post,* January 4, 1998, 21.

Page 59. Betty Smith, quoted in *Happiness Is an Inside Job: Humor & Wisdom Celebrating the Art of Happiness,* created by Meiji Stewart (Del Mar, Calif.: PuddleDancer Press 1997), 76.

Marian Wright Edelman, "Be Your Child's Mentor," *Parade* magazine, October 24, 1999, 10-11.

Joseph Campbell, *The Power of Myth* (New York: Doubleday, 1988), 91.

Page 62. Lorraine Hale, quoted in *Guideposts,* December 1998, 60.

Page 64. Foka Gomez quoted in Mary Engelbreit's *Just for Today, Be Happy 2000 Calendar* entry for September 1, 2000.

Page 65. Ray Ziegler, personal communication to Lee Richmond.

Chapter 4. The Wonder of Space and Time: A Gift to Womanhood

Page 75. Annie Dillard. The source of this quote is unknown.

Page 76. Beverly Elaine Eanes, "Reflections in Our Spiritual Windows," *Currents* 1999 (News & Information, Pastoral Counseling, Loyola College in Maryland); 5.

Jacques L. Leclerq, *The Interior Life,* Fergus Murphy, trans. (New York: P. J. Kenedy & Sons, 1961).

Page 78. May Sarton, quoted in *Sky Magazine,* April 1995 (Delta Airlines), 46.

Page 79. Glen Dromgoole, *What Dogs Teach Us...Life's Lessons Learned from Our Best Friends* (Minocqua, Wis.: Willow Creek Press, 1999), 107.

Beverly Elaine Eanes said this to husband while out walking among the colorful autumn trees near a picturesque lake (October 1999).

Page 80. Thomas Mann, *The Magic Mountain* (1924) translated from the German by H. T. Lowe-Porter (New York: Alfred A. Knopf, 1992), 4.

Page 81. Abraham Joshua Heschel, *I Asked for Wonder* (New York: Crossroad, 1993), 65.

Edna St. Vincent (Millay), "Renascence," in *Collected Poems: Edna St. Vincent Millay*, Norman Millay, ed. (New York: Harper Brothers, 1949), 3-13.

Page 82. Mother Teresa, quoted in Gareri Kinney, "Creating Fulfillment in Today's Workplace: A Guide for Nurses," *American Journal of Nursing* 98, no. 5 (May 1998), 44.

Helen Keller, quoted in *Giving Is Caring Page-A-Day Calendar* entry for January 2, 1989.

Page 83. Anne Morrow Lindbergh, quoted in Stewart, *Happiness is an Inside Job: Humor & Wisdom Celebrating the Art of Happiness*, 56.

Page 85. Tilden Edwards, *Sabbath Time* (Minneapolis: Seabury Press, 1982), 3.

Page 86. Thich Nhat Hanh, *Peace Is Every Step–the Path of Mindfulness in Everyday Life* (New York: Bantam Books, 1991), 44.

Attributed to Mohandas Gandhi. The source of this quote is unknown.

Chapter 5. God, the Sacred and WomanSoul

Page 89. Patricia Hopkins, quoted in Sherry Ruth Anderson and Patricia Hopkins, *The Feminine Face of God: The Unfolding of the Sacred in Women* (New York: Bantam Books, 1991), 4.

Lee J. Richmond, Rex Gallaher, and Kimberly Carney, "Female Spirituality and Careering in the U.S. Postal Service," (unpublished study presented at the American Psychological Association, 107th Annual Conference, Boston, August 1999).

Page 91. Mary McLeod Bethune, quoted in *Guideposts,* November 1996, 37.

Personal Communication, Journal of Sister Margaret Downs S.S.N.D. (entry August 1, 1988, unpublished).

Page 92. Edwin Keith, quoted in *Guideposts,* February 1999, 43.

Notes

Page 93. Virginia Satir, quoted in *Many Strong and Beautiful Women*, 15.

Page 94. Quote on a plaque outside Carl Jung's office and later on his tombstone in Kussnacht, Switzerland.

Page 95. John Macquarrie, *The Principles of Christian Theology*, 2nd ed. (New York: Charles Scribner's Sons, 1977), 329.

Page 96. Jean Shinoda Bolen, quoted in Sherry Ruth Anderson and Patricia Hopkins, *The Feminine Face of God: The Unfolding of the Sacred in Women* (New York: Bantam Books 1992), xi.

Lee J. Richmond, "Gender Differences Across Age in Religiousness and Spirituality," (unpublished paper presented at 23rd Annual Feminist Psychology Conference of the Association for Women in Psychology, Baltimore, March 1998).

Gina Ogden, "Beyond Skin Hunger: Mystical Union in Women's Sexual Relationships" (paper presented at the meeting of the American Psychological Association, Chicago, August 1997).

Edwina Gateley, "I Hear God Laughing," talk given at Mundlein College, Chicago (spring, 1991); audiotape (Trabuco Canyon, Calif.: Source Books, 1991).

Page 97. Anita Roddick, *Full Voice* (booklet, United Kingdom: the Body Shop, 1998), 4-5.

The "Barbie" doll is a product of the Mattel Corporation.

Juliana of Norwich, "Selections from Revelations of Divine Love," *Great Devotional Classics,* Constance Garrett, ed. (Nashville, Tenn.: Upper Room Publishers, 1963), 10.

J. D. Ostrov, as reported by Anne Marshall and Marla Avery, from a study by D. Offer, J. D. Ostrov, K. I. Howard, and R. Atkinson, "Perspectives on Voice and Sense of Self Among Young Adolescents," *School Counselor* 3, no. 1 (October 1999), 44.

Page 98. Kathleen Norris, *The Cloister Walk* (New York: Riverside Books, 1996), 269.

Tanakh: The Holy Scriptures, Song of Songs, 2:1 (Philadelphia: Jewish Publication Society 1985), 1406.

Chapter 6. Discovery, Creativity and Mirth

Page 105. Nadine Stair quoted in Stewart, *Happiness Is an Inside Job: Humor & Wisdom Celebrating the Art of Happiness*, 153.

Page 107. Anne Morrow Lindbergh quoted in *Many Strong and Beautiful Women*, 39.

Robert J. Wicks, *Ordinariness, Spirituality and Self-esteem* (Credence Cassettes, 1993).

Page 108. Germaine de Stael, quoted in *Giving Is Caring Page-A-Day Calendar*, entry for December 16, 1989.

Page 109. Helen Keller, quoted in *Guideposts,* September 1995, 46.

Page 110. Sarah Ban Breathnach, "Learning to Let Go," *Good Housekeeping,* August 1998, 76.

Matthew Fox, *A Spirituality Named Compassion* (Harper SanFrancisco, 1990), 131.

The World Book Dictionary, vol. 2 L–Z, Clarence L. Barnhart and Robert K. Barnhart, ed. (Chicago: Field Enterprises Educational Corporation, 1976), 1897.

Joseph Joubert quoted in Mary Engelbreit's *Just for Today, Be Happy 2000 Calendar,* entry for January 24, 2000.

Page 111. Maria Cooper Janis, "Dear Poppa," *Attaché,* November 1999 (U.S. Airways), 20.

Kahlil Gibran, quoted in Patty Wooten, *Compassionate Laughter: Jest for Your Health* (Salt Lake City: Commune-A-Key Publishing, 1996), 159.

Page 112. Max Lucado, quoted in Stewart, *Happiness Is an Inside Job: Humor & Wisdom Celebrating the Art of Happiness*, 29.

Page 113. Merry Browne, ibid., 109.

Notes

Washington Irving quoted in Stoddard, *Mothers: A Celebration,* 12.

Aimee Mullins quoted in Elizabeth Shepard, " 'Confidence Is the Sexiest Thing a Woman Can Have,' " *Parade* magazine, June 21, 1998, 8, 10.

Mary Kay Ash, quoted in *Happiness Is an Inside Job*, 29.

Page 114. Marie Curie, quoted in *Many Strong and Beautiful Women*, 35.

Page 116. Yitta Halberstam and Judith Leventhal, *Small Miracles of Love & Friendship: Remarkable Coincidences of Warmth & Devotion* (Holbrook, Mass.: Adams Media Corporation, 1999), 40.

Page 118. Anne Wilson Schaef quoted in *Connections: The Health Ministries Association*—Information & Contacts 99, no. 4 (Winter 1999), 7.

Page 119. Serene West, quoted in Patty Wooten, *Compassionate Laughter: Jest for Your Health...*, 1.

Chapter 7. Hope and Healing in the Wider World

Page 127. Marian Wright Edelman, *Guide My Feet: Prayers and Meditations on Loving and Working for Children* (Boston: Beacon Press, 1995), 118.

The reference to Anne Frank's diary in Anne Frank, *The Diary of A Young Girl* (first published in German in 1947 by her father, Otto Frank) 1952; translated from the original German by Otto Frank, Bantam ed. (New York: Bantam Books 1993), 171.

Page 128. Barbara Kingsolver, *Animal Dreams* (New York: HarperCollins, 1990), 299.

Page 129. Ellen Goodman, quoted in *Have a Good Day* (Carol Stream, Ill.: Tyndale House, December 1999), 2.

John Welch, *The Way to Love* (New York: Doubleday Image, 1982), 157.

Page 130. Joni Eareckson Tada, "Wheels for the World Special Report: Turning Castaways into Treasures," *Joni and Friends Newsletter* (March 2000), 1.

Joni Eareckson Tada, *Joni's Story...* (pamphlet, Agoura Hills, Calif.: JAF Ministries), 4.

Page 131. Marian Wright Edelman, "Be Your Child's Mentor," *Parade* magazine, October 24, 1999, 10.

Page 132. Ray Bradbury, quoted in *Guideposts,* March, 1988, 5.

Page 133. Karen Sunde, quoted in Stoddard, *Mothers: A Celebration,* 63.

"The Daughter Track," *Newsweek,* July 16, 1990, cover.

Page 134. Anne Lamott, *Traveling Mercies: Some Thoughts on Faith* (New York: Pantheon Books, 1999), 219.

Tao-te Ching, quoted in Jeanne Carbonetti, *Watercolor: A Revolutionary Approach to the Practice of Painting* (New York: Watson-Guptill Publications, 199), 33.

Page 135. Norman Cousins, *Anatomy of an Illness as Perceived by the Patient* (New York: W.W. Norton & Company, 1979), 27–48.

Page 136. Erma Bombeck, quoted in stories by John William Smith, *Hugs for Mom* (West Monroe, La.: Howard Publishing, 1997), 71.

Grace Noll Crowell, quoted in *Giving is Caring Page-A-Day Calendar,* entry for October 16, 1989.

Page 137. Madeleine L'Engle, quoted in Carole F. Chase, *Madeleine L'Engle, Suncatcher: Spiritual Vision of a Storyteller* (San Diego: Lura-Media, 1995), 104.

Elizabeth Barrett Browning, quoted in *Guideposts,* February 1999, 36.

Page 138. May Sarton, quoted in *Many Strong and Beautiful Women,* 27.

Marcus Borg, *Meeting Jesus Again for the First Time: The Historical Jesus & the Heart of Contemporary Faith* (HarperSanFrancisco, 1994), 87.

Page 139. Anais Nin, quoted in Eugene F. Hemrick, *The Promise of Virtue* (Notre Dame, Ind.: Ave Maria Press, 1999), 112.

Tanakh: The Holy Scriptures, Ecclesiastes 3:1 (Philadelphia: Jewish Publication Society, 1985), 1444.

Page 140. Louise Bogan quoted in Sarah Ban Breathnach, *Simple Abundance: A Daybook of Comfort and Joy* (New York: Warner Books, 1995).

Page 141. Mother Teresa, quoted in Quinn, *Quotable Women of the Twentieth Century,* 6.

Elizabeth O'Conner, *Cry Pain, Cry Hope* (Waco, Tex.: Word Books Publisher, 1987), 99.

Epilogue
Page 144. Albert Schweitzer, quoted in *Guideposts,* January 2000, 38.